Beautiful JUNK II

More Creative Classroom Uses for Recyclable Materials

Karen Brackett and Rosie Manley

Fearon Teacher Aids

Simon & Schuster Education Group

To my Dad for all the love and encouragement he has given me. Also, a special thanks to my husband Bob and my son Bobby who have always been supportive of my dreams.

Karen

To my husband John and my children Shelly and Robbie who have always made collecting beautiful junk a family venture. Thanks for your love, help, and support.

Rosie

Together, to our many years teaching young children and college students at the Center for Child Study, Skidmore College.

Karen and Rosie

Editorial Director: Virginia L. Murphy

Editor: Kristin Eclov

Copyeditor: Lisa Schwimmer

Illustration: Tracy LaRue Hall

Cover and book design: Rose Sheifer

Production: Rebecca Speakes

ISBN 0-86653-937-9

Printed in the United States of America

1. 9 8 7 6 5 4

Printed on Recycled Paper

Contents

 # Preface

For several years, a tight economy and small budgets have forced teachers to look for inexpensive materials to use in their classrooms. Most teachers have closets full of things, such as cardboard tubes, milk cartons, fabric swatches, and wallpaper books. These types of materials challenge children to find unique uses for everyday objects, thereby encouraging divergent and creative thinking. Also, ecological values are communicated to each student as he or she lives and learns in an environment in which conservation of resources, multiple uses of materials, and innovative approaches are everyday practices.

Due to the overwhelming response to our first book on recyclables, and the fact that many programs are faced with economic cutbacks, we decided to put together some additional activities to use with recyclable materials. We hope that you and your students will enjoy using these activities and that our ideas will encourage creative thinking to produce an endless supply of possibilities.

Sources of Free and Inexpensive Materials

In order to obtain optimal cooperation from suppliers of "junk," we have found that it is important to

1. make personal contacts,
2. go back frequently, and
3. provide your own container for collection.

HOME

Newspapers, wrapping paper, greeting cards, scrap paper, milk cartons, baby food jars, egg cartons, cereal boxes, oatmeal boxes, jello and pudding boxes, plastic lids, coffee cans with lids, juice cans with lids, metal fruit and vegetable cans, cardboard backs to tablets, yarn, string, fabric scraps, wood scraps, hair color and permanent squeeze bottles, leftover paint, buttons, beads, popsicle sticks, thread spools, twist ties, nutshells, old crayons, seeds, dress-up clothes, paper towel and toilet tissue tubes, detergent containers, old cookie sheets and baking pans, magazines, empty plastic bottles, cigar boxes, shoeboxes, gift boxes, catalogs, 35-mm film containers, junk mail, old keys, paper bags, Styrofoam trays, six pack plastic rings, pizza boxes, berry baskets, corks, game pieces and dice, canceled stamps, old calendars, soda containers, dryer lint, plastic frosting tubs, deodorant roller bottles, clothespins

NATURE

Feathers, stones and pebbles, tree bark, apple and watermelon seeds, acorns and maple tree seeds, sand, seashells, dried grass clippings, leaves, mosses and ferns, pine needles, cherry and peach pits, sticks and twigs, dried weeds, such as milkweed pods, cattails, dockweed, pinecones

SCHOOLS/OFFICE/CAFETERIA

Old calendars, Styrofoam packing pieces, Styrofoam peanuts, newspapers, computer paper ends, copy machine rolls, cardboard backs of notebooks, scrap paper, canceled stamps, old envelopes, catalogs and junk mail, scrap paper and magazines, milk cartons, plastic tubs and jugs

GROCERY STORES

Packing and shipping separators for samples, fruit and vegetable dividers, weekly advertisements, cardboard boxes, leftover display items, yogurt container trays

BUSINESSES

Card shops—old cards and envelopes; paint stores—sample paint, old color charts; packing stores—damaged cartons, various cardboard scraps; florist—ribbon, foam, wire; fabric stores—fabric, yarn, buttons, lace, fabric samples, thread spools, and cardboard fabric rolls; lumber stores—wood scraps, building material scraps, sawdust, wood curls; feed store—burlap sacks, seed catalogs, seeds; carpet stores—carpet samples; wallpaper stores—wallpaper sample books, wallpaper scraps; furniture stores—fabric, linoleum scraps, floor tile, drapery samples, brochures, upholstery samples; drugstores—35-mm film containers; department stores—catalogs; tile stores—discontinued or broken tiles; liquor stores—heavy boxes, cardboard displays; photographers—35-mm film containers, picture folders; newspaper—newsprint, scrap paper, 35-mm film containers, newspaper.

Boxes

1. RECYCLABLE ART CENTER

Collect eight large boxes with top flaps.
Cut off one long flap and the two shorter side
flaps from each box. Tape the remaining long
flap to the box creating a pocket. Arrange the
boxes so the flaps are on the bottom. Tape
the boxes together and cover with contact
paper. Fill the art center with colored paper
scraps, yarn, ribbons, empty small boxes, old
greeting cards, old notebook covers, newspaper inserts, comics, empty plastic bottles,
and so on.

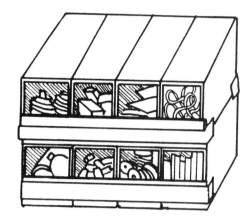

2. PRIVACY SCREENS

Cardboard boxes can make great privacy screens for test-taking, or whenever a
student would like more privacy during work time. To make the screens, use
boxes slightly smaller than the surface of a student's desk. Cut off the top, bottom, and one long side of each box—the three remaining sides should be connected together. Stand the screen on the desk so that the long side is toward the
back of the desk and the shorter sides give privacy at the sides.

3. REPORT DISPLAYS

Use pizza boxes as displays for state reports.
Make salt maps of the states in the bottoms.
Attach the written reports to the inside lids.
Use picture corners to hold the reports in
place. Decorate the outside of the boxes with
newspaper and magazine pictures and words
associated with each state.

4. ALL ABOUT ME SUPPLY BOXES

Have students cover empty tissue boxes with pictures and words cut from
magazines and newspapers. Choose pictures that tell something about each student, such as favorite foods, clothing, sports, pets, and other interests. Invite each
student to keep his or her supplies in a personalized box.

5. BOOK AND PAPER HOLDER

Cut the top off a large detergent box. Mark the sides with diagonal lines—from the top corner to the bottom. Cut along the line on each side. Cover with contact paper. Use the book and paper holder to store teacher guides, papers, folders, workbooks, and so on.

6. BOOKENDS

Fill empty oatmeal boxes with sand. Securely tape the lid of the box and then cover the whole cylinder with contact paper. Decorate with stickers or colored tape.

7. PLACE VALUE

Find numbers with certain place values, such as 10,000s or 0.100s, on labels of empty food boxes.

Variation: Compare the percentages, weights, and daily requirements of vitamins on the different product labels.

8. GEOMETRY

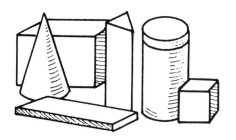

Categorize boxes by shape—cylinders, cones, cubes, rectangular prisms, and so on. Cut boxes into two-dimensional shapes, such as circles, squares, or rectangles. Write the names of the shapes inside or on the back for self-checking.

9. SODA CASE SHADOW BOXES

Use shallow, soft drink case boxes as a base for shadow box pictures. Glue a variety of materials to the box to create scenes for stories or books. For outdoor pictures, spread glue on the inside of the box and then sprinkle with sand. When the glue is covered, pour off excess sand. Students can also use small sticks, grass clippings, pinecones, construction paper, cardboard, and plastic items to decorate the shadow boxes.

Variation: Decorate a cardboard box with heavy cardboard dividers. Use the box as a storage area for lightweight objects, such as small plastic figurines from fast-food restaurants.

10. SIX FOOD GROUPS

You'll need six large boxes for this activity. Designate one box for each of the six categories of the FDA Food Pyramid: dairy; meat, fish, poultry, and nuts; fruits; vegetables; grains; and sugars and fats. (For an example of the pyramid, refer to American Teaching Aids' chart ATA 2165 *The Nutrition Pyramid*. For a catalog, call 1-800-423-6537.) Have students place empty food containers or labels of foods in the proper boxes. Put a sticker on each container that is especially high in nutritional value.

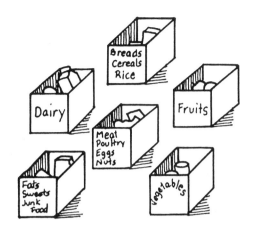

Detergent, Hair Spray, and Spray Starch Caps

1. FLORAL BOUQUET

Fold a 9" x 12" piece of green construction paper in half lengthwise. Cut slits one inch apart starting at the fold and stopping short of 2 inches of the opposite edge. Push one edge of the paper up approximately one inch, keeping the sides lined up. Staple the edges in place. This will cause the "leaves" to bend. Roll the paper tightly so the paper strips bend to the outside like leaves. Tuck the bouquet into the plastic detergent or hair spray cap and glue if necessary. Paste crumpled pieces of colored tissue paper onto the leaves to look like flowers. These are especially nice for Mother's Day or Father's Day. Add a card stapled to a popsicle stick or straw to complete the floral gift.

2. RECIPE CARD HOLDER

Fill a hair spray cap almost full with plaster of paris. Before it sets, place a plastic fork, handle edge down and slightly tilted, into the plaster. After the plaster has hardened, glue plastic or silk flowers or greenery around the edge of the fork. Place a recipe card in the tines of the fork for easy viewing. Have each child dictate his or her favorite recipe, complete with directions.

3. CIRCLE PRINTING

Use cap edges dipped in paint for printing circles. Use the cap tops for printing solid circles. You can also glue a variety of materials, such as felt, sponges, cardboard or inner tubing, to the cap tops to create interesting shapes for printing.

4. CANDLE HOLDER

Fill a plastic detergent or spray starch cap almost full with plaster of paris. Before it sets, place a candle in the plaster. Decorate around the base of the candle with such items as real evergreens, small plastic ornaments or candy canes to celebrate the holidays, or flowers and green leaves for spring, or fall leaves and acorns for autumn. (Decorations can be glued in place after the plaster dries or pushed directly into the plaster before it hardens.)

5. PLAYDOUGH CUTTER

Have an adult drill a small hole in the top of a plastic cap to allow for air to escape. Use different-sized caps with playdough or as stencils to make perfect circles. Clean plastic caps can also be used as cookie cutters for real baking.

6. PLANTER

Drill several holes in the top of liquid laundry detergent caps. Place several pebbles or small Styrofoam chips before adding dirt to allow for better drainage for plants. Place a plastic margarine lid under each plant to catch the excess water. This size planter is great for starting seeds. They also are a nice size for small spring plants like marigolds and alyssum.

Variation: Buy paper white narcissus bulbs from your local florist. Fill caps partway with small rocks. Aquarium rocks are a good size. Place the bulb on top of the rocks and fill in spaces around the bulb with more rocks for extra support. Add water so that the base of the bulb is touching it. Keep in a sunny location and be prepared to enjoy a little bit of spring indoors while winter continues outside.

7. MOUSE PAINT

Read the book *Mouse Paint* by Ellen Stohl Walsh (Orlando, FL: Harcourt, Brace, Jovanovich, 1989). Set up a painting table with several work areas, each with its own set of three plastic caps—one red, one yellow and one blue, each containing the corresponding colors of paint. Allow the children free opportunity for paint mixing on a surface before giving them paper to paint on. Old cookie sheets, plastic picnic plates, microwave dishes, or large Styrofoam meat trays are great because the paint does not absorb and thereby allows the children the full freedom to mix and remix before painting a final product. Encourage the students to experiment with different painting techniques. Allow the finished products to dry completely before handling.

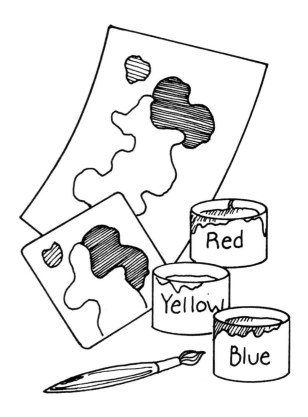

Variation: Make prints directly from the mixing tray by laying the paper on the tray, rubbing gently across the back of the paper and lifting the paper to achieve a "monoprint." Thus the children could continue to mix and print before cleaning the tray.

8. BUBBLE BLOWERS

Drill several large holes in a hair spray cap. Dip the top of the cap in bubble solution or diluted dishwashing liquid. Have the children create mounds of beautiful bubble clusters by waving the bubble blowers through the air.

9. HOLIDAY CANDLE

Mix up a batch of whipped snow by beating together 1 1/2 cups of Ivory Snow and 1 cup of water. Paint or pat the snow mixture onto a eight-inch long paper-towel tube. Sprinkle the snow-covered tube with glitter if desired. Glue the tube in place inside the plastic hair spray cap. Allow the glue to dry before adding the decorations. Decorate around the base of the tube with evergreens, felt holly pieces, or small holiday decorations. Cut a "flame" from gold foil and glue to the inside of the top edge of the candle.

 # Egg Cartons

1. HOLIDAY WREATH

Cut an egg carton bottom into two long 6-cup sections. Cut small slits between cups along the outside edge to allow the section to curve. Staple the ends together to form a circle. Arrange the circle on a piece of cardboard with the outside of the egg carton facing up and staple in place. Trim around the outside edge of the egg carton circle. If possible, cut around the inside of the egg carton circle, too. Paint the wreath green and decorate with a red bow, red pom-poms or pieces of crushed red tissue paper.

Variation: Cut a toilet paper tube in half lengthwise. Paint or cover the tube with colored construction paper. Cut small slits in the bottom of the tube and slide onto the inner edge of the cardboard circle to look like a candle inside the wreath. Add a foil or tissue flame.

2. CLOCK

Use the same procedure as the holiday wreath, but do not cut an inner circle in the cardboard base. Cut clock hands out of construction paper. Attach the hands to the center of the cardboard base with a brass fastener. Glue numbered circles to the egg cup sections to represent the numbers on a clock face.

3. CREATURE FEATURES

Cut a 2-cup section from the egg carton bottom and include the raised section seperating the two rows of cups. This will be the eyes and nose of a creature. Glue the egg cup section to a paper plate, box, or circle and add details to create a real or imaginary creature. For example, add ears and whiskers to create a mouse. Challenge students to come up with their own ideas.

4. BINOCULARS

Cut a 2-cup section from the end of an egg carton bottom. Trim away the raised section separating the two rows of cups so the binoculars will fit over the nose. Cut out the small circles at the bottom of the cup sections for children to look through. Attach a string to the sides so the binoculars can hang around the children's necks.

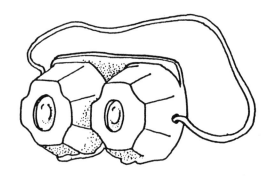

Variation: Cover the open circles at the end of the binoculars with colored cellophane to make colored glasses.

5. CATERPILLAR

Cut out the long raised section from the egg carton lid. Paint the section to look like a caterpillar and let it dry overnight. Glue a large pom-pom to the first opening of the lid for the caterpillar's head. Add pipe cleaners for antennae and eyes and other details. Glue small pom-poms, crumpled tissue paper, or colored paper circles to the raised portions of the carton to complete the caterpillar.

6. EGG CARTON SCULPTURES

Cut apart cardboard egg carton cups in varying combinations—6-cup long sections, 4-cup square sections, and so on. Allow children to glue sections randomly on heavy cardboard bases. If possible, provide a variety of colors of egg cartons.

Variation: Allow interested children to paint the sculptures. The paper cartons "hold" the paint very well and little nooks and crannies of the cartons are fun to paint.

7. CROWN

Each egg carton bottom will make two crowns. Cut the egg carton in half lengthwise. Then cut one section in half again to create two long pieces. Staple the two sections together to make a circle, with the inside of the egg cups facing out. Decorate the crown with pieces of foil or crumpled tissue-paper jewels.

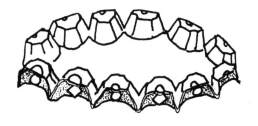

8. SPRING FLOWERS

Trim around the top of one egg cup section to make four petals for a tulip. Paint and add a pipe cleaner stem and stamen. Glue the egg carton flower on paper and add painted leaves to the stem.

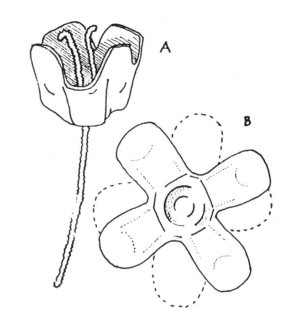

Variation: Using two egg cup sections, trim the edges and cut the petals all the way to the bottom so that the four petals for each egg cup will lay flat. Glue one section on top of the other to form an eight-petaled flower. Paint the flower. Add a pipe cleaner stem and a colorful pom-pom to the center. Glue the flowers to construction paper.

9. EGG CARTON BIRD FEEDER

Remove the lid from the egg carton. Cut the bottom carton into two sections with six egg cups each. Fill the cups with birdseed. If possible, place the bird feeders on a window-sill or in a tree outside the classroom so students can observe the wildlife activity.

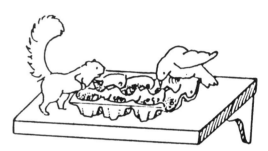

10. MANIPULATIVE MULTIPLICATION

Cut the tops off six egg cartons. Arrange the six bottoms in a box to create six rows of twelve egg cups. Use dried beans or seeds to demonstrate multiplication principles. Encourage students to use the egg cartons for independent practice.

11. NAMEPLATE

Cut apart the bottoms of several egg cartons. Turn the individual cups upside down and line up as many sections as letters in each student's name. Cut out letters from magazines and newspapers and glue to the bottoms of the egg cups. Glue the egg cups to heavy construction paper to create a nameplate for each student.

12. SANTA

Cut apart two connected cups from an egg carton. Fold the cups towards each other and staple the edges. Repeat with two more connected cups. Glue the two stapled shapes together. Decorate with red paint, construction paper, fabric scraps, glitter, and cotton balls for a beard.

13. HOT-AIR BALLOON

Cut a balloon shape from construction paper (see the pattern provided on page 17). Decorate the balloon with watercolors, crayons, markers, and so on. Cut one egg cup section from a carton bottom. Trim the edges to form a scalloped edge. Punch a hole in two sides of the egg cup with a paper punch. Thread a piece of string through each hole in the balloon basket. Knot the string ends together and tape them to the back of the balloon shape. Decorate a wooden ice-cream spoon to look like a person and glue it inside the balloon basket.

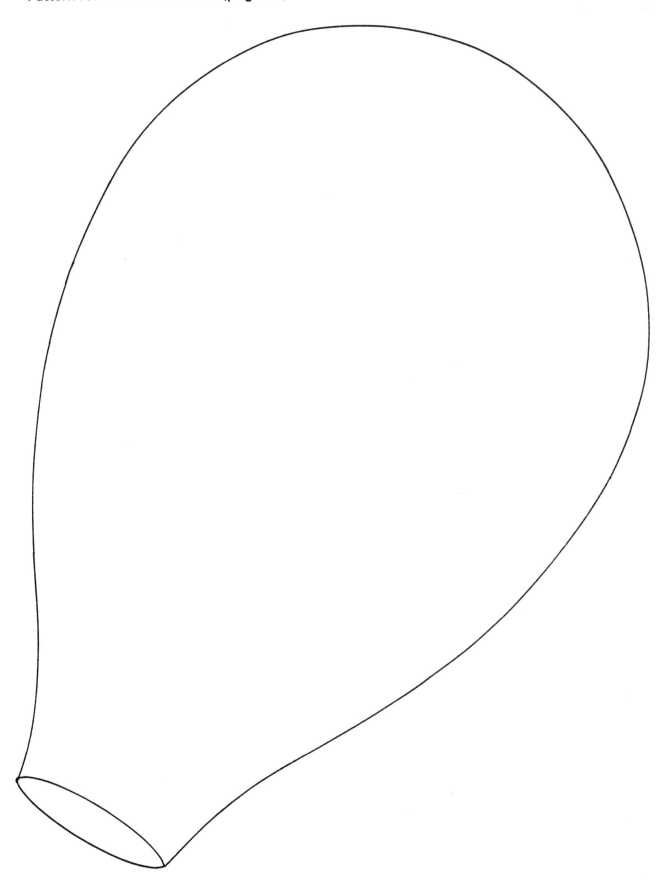

FABRIC

1. PUFFY PAINT ON FABRIC

Glue (craft glue works best for this part of the project) an 8" x 10" section of solid colored fabric to a piece of heavy cardboard. Allow to dry overnight. To make puffy paint, mix equal parts of flour, salt, and water. Add a little Elmer's glue and food coloring to the mixture. Mix up several different colors of puffy paint and put the mixtures into small, empty squeeze bottles, such as bottles used for hair coloring products, or old glue bottles. Have the children squeeze a variety of colors of puffy paint onto the material board. As the paint dries, it puffs up. These look great displayed.

2. CORDUROY BEARS

Read the story *Corduroy* by Don Freeman (New York: Viking Press, 1968). As a follow-up activity, have the children make their own Corduroy bears (see the patterns on pages 19-20). Have buttons, yarn scraps, markers, and wallpaper pieces available for facial features.

3. SPECIAL CARDS

Cut out hearts with different designs to use on the cover of a special card. Glue the hearts to the front of the card and write the following poem inside to help celebrate Mother's or Father's Day. Use an oaktag weight paper.

Wishful Thinking

I wish on this special Mother's (Father's) Day,

That you may do what you want to do.

And I just want to say,

You're a great Mom (Dad) and I love you!

Happy Mother's (Father's) Day !

Love,

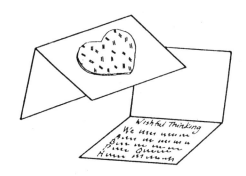

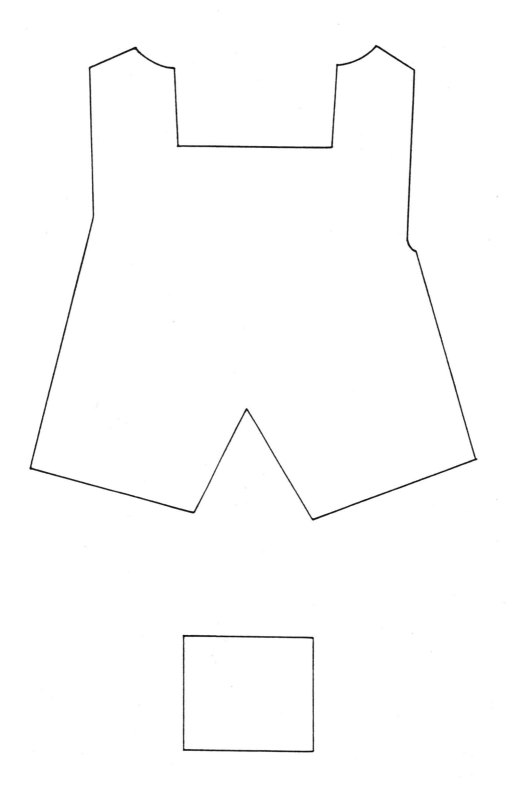

4. WE DRESS FOR WEATHER DOLLS

Cut out a doll from oaktag or heavy construction paper (see the pattern on page 22). Provide different kinds of fabric pieces to make clothes for the dolls. This activity stimulates great discussions about seasons. It's also fun to have the children dictate stories about their dolls.

5. STYROFOAM TREES

Have Styrofoam cones and 1 1/2" wreath pins available for this activity. Cut fabric into 1" x 1" squares with pinking shears. Have the children attach the material squares to the Styrofoam with the wreath pins. Continue to overlap the fabric until the cone is completely covered.

Variation: Styrofoam wreath shapes can be covered in the same way.

6. LEAF HANGING

Use a large piece of fabric or an old sheet to create a class leaf hanging. Bring in several large pieces of wood to use as a work surface. Place newspaper on top of the wood, then a green leaf, then cover the leaf with a section of the cloth. Using a hammer, pound the leaf through the cloth. As the leaf is pounded, it will release the green chlorophyll to form a leaf imprint on the cloth. Use a variety of leaf sizes and shapes to make the hanging more interesting. Several children can work on this project at a time.

Note: The authors have experimented with using fall leaves that are just beginning to change colors. They have found that the colors that are produced on the fabric are not as bright or well defined as they are with the green leaves.

7. FABRIC DOMINOES

Glue (craft glue works best with fabric) two 2" x 2" squares of material onto a 2" x 4" piece of cardboard. Vary your patterns to make at least 20 cards. Have the children take turns matching the patterns until all the cards are used.

Pattern for "We Dress for Weather Dolls" (page 21)

8. BRAIDING

Cut pieces of fabric into 2-inch wide strips. Sew three strips together at one end for easier handling. Have the children braid the strips together. Make mini-rugs for a dollhouse by coiling the braid and sewing the braided strips together.

9. T-SHIRT PILLOWS

Collect old, small T-shirts. Ask a parent volunteer to help students sew the sleeves and neck openings closed. Stuff the T-shirts with batting and stitch the bottoms. Decorate the pillows with fabric paint, if desired. Use the pillows in a reading center.

10. CLASS QUILT

Give each child a 12" square of solid colored material and have him or her decorate the square with fabric paint designs or hand-prints. Have parents volunteer to help sew the squares together to make the top of the quilt. Then insert the batting for the middle, and add a bed sheet for the backing. Sew the outside edges together. Then tie the corners of each square to hold all the layers together. Display for all to enjoy!

11. LACY CEDAR BALLS

Cut a circle of lace or netting about 8" in diameter. Put a handful or two of clean cedar chips (purchased from a pet store) inside the lace circles. Gather together the sides around the cedar chips and secure the edges with a rubberband. Tie with ribbon.

Variation: Place potpourri or cloves in a five-inch square of pretty scrap fabric. Tie with ribbon or yarn. Hang in a room, or place in a clothes drawer.

12. BANNER

Glue, sew, or paint designs, mottoes, or names on rectangular pieces of fabric. Attach the pieces of fabric to dowels or broom handles. Display the banners in the classroom.

13. CHARACTER HATS

Bring in old, plain fabric hats. Dip thumbs into the fabric paint and firmly press onto the hats. Use a fine-tip paintbrush to create thumbprint characters.

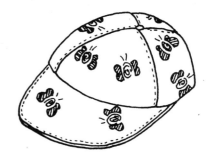

14. FRINGE T-SHIRT

Bring in old T-shirts. Cut slits approximately 5" long and ½" wide around the bottoms of the shirts. Tie knots at the top and at the bottom of the fringed pieces.

15. TIE-DYE PAINTING

Use old tie-dyed T-shirts as backgrounds for painting. Place heavy cardboard inside the T-shirt as a hard painting surface. Create designs on the T-shirts with black fabric paint and fine paintbrushes.

16. HAND PAINTED T-SHIRTS

Have children bring in old, plain colored T-shirts that may have permanent stains on them. Use sponge paintbrushes and fabric paint to make handprints or footprints or other designs on the T-shirts. Allow the paint prints to dry overnight. Follow the directions on the fabric paint to iron the hand painted originals.

Film Canisters and Other Small Plastic Bottles

Small plastic bottles with caps, such as pill bottles or 35-mm film canisters, will work well with most of these activities. Film canisters can be obtained from parents, film developers, professional photographers, or even your local newspapers. Canisters and lids can be clear or opaque.

1. SNIFFERS

Drill or melt five holes in the lids of several opaque film canisters. Number the bottoms of the canisters and make numbered cards to set along side. Place one item with a scent in each canister and replace the lid. Have students sniff the items and try to guess the contents. Ideas for the sniffer canisters might include onions, garlic, gum, oranges, instant coffee, mustard, ketchup, pickles, cinnamon, baby powder, perfume, peppermint oil, spices, and so on.

2. SOUND MATCH

Fill pairs of opaque film canisters or pill bottles with items that make distinct sounds when shaken, such as rice, sand, water, small bells, or pennies. Replace the canister lids and start shaking. Arrange the canisters on a table in random order. Shake the canisters to find the two sounds that match. Write matching numbers on the bottoms of the different pairs for self-checking.

3. COLOR SORTING

Fill several clear canisters with colored water. Have at least two containers of each color. Glue the lids in place. Ask the children to group the containers by color. Provide two or more canisters filled with water to help the students understand the absence of color.

4. RATTLES

Decorate the outside of 35-mm film canisters with markers, stickers, fabric, and so on. Drill or melt holes in the bottoms of the canisters large enough to snugly fit popsicle-stick handles. Push the handles through the holes and glue around the outside to keep the popsicle-sticks secure. Place rice, beans or gravel in the canisters. Add glue around the tops of the canisters and push the lids back on. Use the shakers as rhythm instruments.

5. SEASONAL TREES

Glue 35-mm film canisters to 5" x 5" heavy bases, such as oaktag. Partially fill the containers with plaster of paris. When the plaster is almost set, firmly push in twigged tree branches. Allow the plaster to dry completely. Decorate the trees according to the season.

Winter—Brush glue on the branches and cover with small pieces of cotton balls or fiberfill. Glue around the bases of the containers and add more cotton to complete the wintry trees.

Autumn—Brush glue on the branches and decorate with crumpled pieces of yellow, red, and orange tissue paper to represent the changing leaves. Add a few tissue-paper leaves to the base to complete the Fall trees.

Spring—Brush glue on the branches and decorate with varied shades of green crumpled tissue paper to represent new leaves. Use the tissue paper around the base to represent new grass growing.

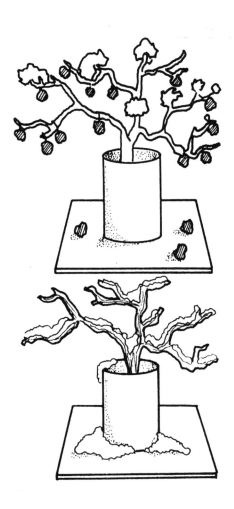

6. COLOR MIXING

Create new colors by mixing small amounts of colored water in clear 35-mm film canisters. Give each child three or four canisters to experiment with. Use eyedroppers to add the colors together. Provide a large pan for easy dumping and remixing.

7. SERIATION ACTIVITIES

Seriation is arranging items in a series according to a property, such as weight, size, or color. The following activities are geared to help students develop this important cognitive skill.

Least to Most—Use clear film canisters filled with colored water, starting with a small amount in the first and gradually increasing the amount in each canister until the last canister is filled completely. Use rubber cement to glue on the lids. Arrange the canisters in order from the least amount of water to the most.

Lightest to Heaviest—Fill several canisters with increasing amounts of a heavy material, such as pennies. Sort the containers by their weight—from lightest to heaviest. Number the bottoms for self-checking. Encourage students to check their guesses using a scale.

Variation: Arrange two matched sets of heavy canisters. Ask children to find the pairs that weigh the same. Have students check their guesses by using a balance scale.

8. RAIN GAUGE

Glue a clear 35-mm film canister to a block of wood. Mark the side of the container with a permanent marker or masking tape in ¼-inch increments. Place the rain gauge outside in an unobstructed area. Monitor the amount of precipitation on a daily, weekly, or monthly basis, depending on where you are located.

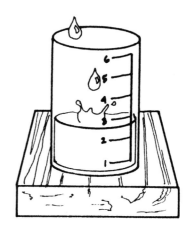

9. SAND PAINTING

Fill clear 35-mm film canisters with layers of different colored sand. Experiment with creating interesting effects by pushing pencils down the inside edges of the containers to create peaks and valleys in the sand. Fill the containers to the top with sand and glue on the lids.

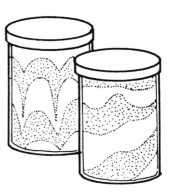

Frozen Juice Can Lids

Use lids from frozen juice cans with the plastic tear strips. These lids have perfectly smooth edges and are not in any way dangerous to children. Use the flatter side, which faces the inside of the can, to attach pins and magnets. Use the raised edge side as the front.

1. BADGES

Attach a safety pin to the back of the lid using a strip of masking tape. Design a variety of paper covers to glue onto the front of the badges. Cover the badge with clear contact paper or laminate before gluing to the metal badge base.

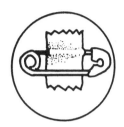

Job Badges—At the beginning of school, prepare badges for student helpers, such as Calendar, Helper, Weather Watcher, Line Leader, Snack Person, Paper Patrol, Messenger, and so on.
Birthday Badges—Make special badges for students to wear on their birthdays.
Award Pins—Make badges to recognize outstanding performance in school, such as Math Whiz, Spelling Ace, Super Friend, Super Helper, Student of the Day, Work Whiz, and so on.

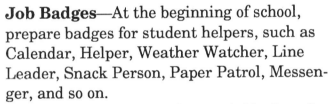

2. COASTERS

Collect four frozen juice can lids. Cut felt circles to fit the inside of the lids. Decorate the other sides of the coasters with flat sequins, fabric, felt, and markers. Stack the four coasters and tie a ribbon around them and give as a gift.

3. TRAFFIC LIGHTS

Paint four juice can lids red, four lids yellow, and four lids green. Glue one set of lids on each side of a ½-gallon milk carton—red lids at the top, yellow lids in the middle, and green lids on the bottom. Punch a hole in the top of the carton and hang from the ceiling.

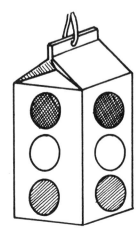

4. PHOTO PINS

Tape a safety pin to the back of juice can lids. Cut photographs of students to fit inside the lids and glue the pictures onto the lids. Photo pins make nice gifts for any occasion.

5. PAPERWEIGHTS

Take a nature walk to collect special rocks and stones. Use juice can lids as bases and invite students to glue the stones closely together. Some children may wish to pile the stones, while others may try to arrange the stones in a pattern. Use plenty of glue to hold the stones in place. It is very important to allow enough time for the paperweights to dry completely before sending home.

Variation: Use a variety of dried beans to create designs.

6. MAGNETS

Glue 2-inch lengths of magnetic strip to the back of the juice can lids to create all types of magnets.

Spelling Practice—Follow the same procedure as above. Then write alphabet letters on the fronts of the lids. Include extra letters to encourage students to practice their spelling words. The magnetic letters can also be used for spelling or reading games to give additional practice in word recognition.

Flower Magnet—Paint the fronts of the lids with colorful glossy paint. Glue construction paper, felt, or fabric petals to the backs of the lids.

7. WIND CHIMES

Use plastic margarine-tub lids or coffee-can lids as bases for wind chimes. Punch three or four holes along the lower edges of the plastic lids. Attach a 10-inch length of string to each hole. Decorate three or four juice can lids with markers, stickers, and glitter. Tape a juice can lid to the end of each string. Punch a hole in the top of each plastic lid and tie a string to hang the wind chimes from the ceiling or a tree branch.

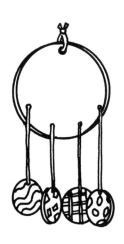

8. NECKLACES

Have an adult volunteer punch a hole in the front of each juice can lid with a nail. Turn the lids over and flatten any raised metal edges around the holes. Cover the holes with masking tape, and then punch holes through the center of the tape. Decorate the lids with glitter, paint, markers, construction paper, fabric scraps, and so on. Thread yarn through the holes to make necklaces.

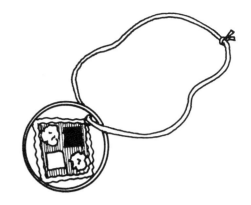

9. STAMPER

Glue small blocks of wood to the front of the juice can lids for handles. Press the backs of the lids onto sponge-paint pads and press onto paper to print perfect circles. Glue felt or sponge shapes to the backs of the lids to make interesting prints.

10. RHYTHM INSTRUMENTS

Create a rhythm band with the following:

Chimes—Have an adult volunteer punch a hole in the front of each juice can lid with a nail. Turn the lids over and flatten any raised metal edges around the holes. Cover the holes with masking tape, then punch a hole through the center of the tape. Hang the lids from string and hit the juice can lid chimes with spoons.

Jingle Lids—Have an adult volunteer punch a hole in three juice can lids with a nail. Turn the lids over and flatten any raised metal edges around the holes. Cover each hole with masking tape, then punch a hole through the center of the tape. Hang all three lids on a piece of yarn and tie the yarn ends together. Shake the jingle lids.

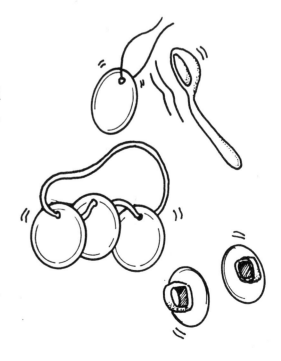

Cymbals—Collect two juice can lids for each pair of cymbals. Glue small pieces of wood to the back of each lid as a handle. Experiment with hitting the lids together.

Finger Cymbals—Glue felt circles or loops to the backs of four lids. Wear a finger cymbal on each thumb and forefinger, then hit the lids together. Experiment with wearing the cymbals on different fingers, too.

 # HEAVY CARDBOARD AND MATBOARD SCRAPS

1. MONKEY PUPPETS

Cut out several monkey puppets from medium-weight cardboard, such as the back of a notebook (see the pattern on page 33). Decorate the monkey puppets with felt pieces and wiggly eyes. Read the story *Caps For Sale* by Esphyr Slobodkina (New York: HarperCollins, 1947) to the class. Have the students use the monkey puppets to dramatize the story.

2. SAND & SHELL COLLAGE

Glue a variety of shells to a matboard base. Sprinkle pinches of sand over any remaining glue spots. Wait several minutes before shaking off the excess sand. Dictate or write stories about trips to the beach. Display the stories and collages in the classroom.

3. ROBOTS

Provide students with a variety of sizes and colors of cardboard scraps to design their own robots. Use other materials to add details to the robots, such as buttons, wallpaper pieces, rickrack, metallic paper scraps, and small wood scraps.

4. VEHICLES

Provide a variety of cardboard pieces for the students to use to design and construct their own vehicles. Glue wood or cardboard wheels on the vehicles and allow to dry overnight. Then paint the cardboard creations with brightly colored tempera paint.

5. MOON CRATERS

Mix ½ cup of liquid starch with 2 cups rock salt and ½ cup glue. Add a few drops of food coloring. The consistency of this mixture will be gooey. Pour the crater mixture onto a heavy piece of cardboard and allow the mixture to dry until hard.

6. PRINT MAKING

Cut pieces of cardboard into various shapes and glue the shapes onto cardboard backing. Use brayers to spread printing ink over the raised surfaces. Carefully place a piece of paper over the inked surfaces and smooth out the wrinkles. Gently lift off the paper and let dry. Mount the design on colored construction paper.

7. PEBBLE MOSAIC

Ask students and their families to help collect small pebbles for this activity. Give each student a 5" x 7" piece of heavy cardboard or wood. Have glue and plenty of different pebbles available. Show students how to glue the pebbles next to each other to completely cover the whole board making a creative mosaic design. Allow students to work on this project for several days.

8. BASE FOR CREATIONS

Use heavy cardboard pieces and matboard scraps for mounting pictures and sculptures.

9. CHALKBOARD STENCILS

Cut several large vehicle shapes out of heavy cardboard. Glue a 3" x 3" Styrofoam block to the back of each shape for a handle. Trace the vehicle shapes on the chalkboard. Use the Styrofoam handles to hold the stencils in place. The stencils can also be used with butcher paper.

Variation: Create stencils of other shapes, such as endangered animals, birds, countries of the world, and so on. These would be great for bulletin-board patterns.

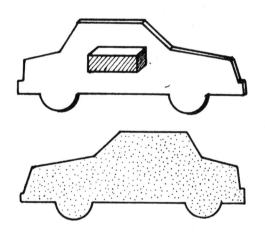

10. RELIEF PICTURE

Glue magazine pictures to heavy cardboard. Cut out the pictures and glue them to a painted background to create a two-dimensional effect.

11. JIGSAW PUZZLE

When photos are taken during the year, save a group picture of your class for this project. Glue the photo with rubber cement to a piece of heavy cardboard—the same size as the picture. Allow the glue to dry completely. Cover both sides of the photograph with laminating film or clear contact paper. Use an X-acto knife to cut curving lines to make puzzle pieces. Be careful not to cut the pieces too small.

12. BEAN WREATH

Cut wreath shapes out of heavy cardboard. Provide a variety of different kinds of dried beans, such as lima, kidney, black beans, and so on. Mix the beans in a large bowl with a craft product called *Modge Podge*. Spoon a thin layer of the bean mixture onto the cardboard shape. Allow the wreath to dry overnight. For a final touch, add a bow for decoration.

Variation: Use other cardboard shapes, such as baskets, leaves, birds, and so on.

 # NEWSPAPER

1. WEAVING

Cut newspaper in long strips. Demonstrate how to weave the strips into rectangular shapes. Cover the woven mats with laminating film or clear contact paper to make placemats.

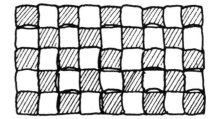

2. WORD COLLAGE

Cut a variety of words out of the newspaper, such as adjectives, nouns, animal names, geographical names, and so on. Glue the words to pieces of construction paper in random patterns.

Variation: Have students write stories using the words cut out of the newspaper. Use this activity to practice identifying parts of speech.

3. BALLOON ORNAMENT

Blow up small balloons. Cover the balloons with a papier-mâché mixture and newspaper strips. To make the papier-mâché, mix together 1 cup of flour and 1 cup of water. After the ornaments are completely dry, paint them with watercolor or tempera paint. Hang the ornaments from the ceiling for a festive holiday atmosphere.

4. TORN PAPER COLLAGE

Tear newspaper into pieces to use on collages. Glue the newspaper pieces onto oaktag. Staple construction paper to the backs of the collages as frames.

5. LOG HOUSES

Create newspaper logs by tightly rolling 2" x 4" pieces of newspaper around pencils. Tape the ends of each log. Use posterboard as the foundation for each log house. Carefully glue the newspaper logs together and allow to dry overnight. Paint the log houses and add details to the surrounding areas.

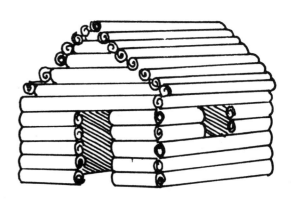

6. LETTER WEEK

Focus on a letter of the alphabet each week. Provide several newspapers for the children to find words or pictures that begin with the letter chosen. Glue the words or pictures to construction paper. After completing the entire alphabet, combine each student's letter pages into a book.

7. STENCIL PAINTING

Paint on large newspaper shapes (see Chalk-board Stencils activity for directions for making large shapes on page 34). Provide a variety of shapes to represent a theme or unit the class is working on, such as transportation, endangered animals, and so on.

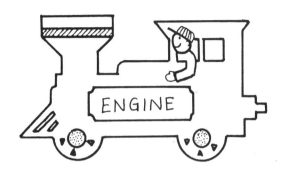

8. PRINTING WITH SILLY PUTTY

Use the following recipe for making silly putty. Experiment with using silly putty to try and reprint the comics from the newspaper. Mix two parts glue with one part starch—gradually pouring the starch into the glue. Add more starch if needed to keep the mixture from getting too sticky. Cover the silly putty and chill overnight.

9. HAND-PAINTED WRAPPING PAPER

Lay out full sheets of newspaper on the floor. Give each student an old sponge to cut into shapes for printing. Dip the sponge shapes in tempera paint. Have students lightly print designs on their newspaper. Allow the designs to dry flat overnight. Use the hand-painted newspaper as wrapping paper for special occasions. Create gift cards to match.

10. FLOOR SQUARES

Use two 12" x 18" pieces of fabric for each floor square. Have children decorate one side of each square, explaining that the sides with the designs will be the tops and bottoms of the mats. Place several layers of folded newspaper between the two pieces of fabric—decorated sides facing outward. Sew around the edges to create a decorated padded mat for sitting on the floor or the ground.

11. BIG BOOK

Write and illustrate familiar or original stories on pieces of construction paper. Glue the stories and pictures to sheets of newspaper and staple the pages together into a big book.

12. NEWSPAPER WRAPPING PAPER

Save the comics sections from Sunday newspapers. Use the colorful comics as wrapping paper for special gifts. Create gift cards with cartoon characters to match. The people receiving the gifts will enjoy reading the wrapping paper as much as opening the gifts!

# Miscellaneous

1. BUBBLE PRINTS

Save bubble packaging material to make bubble prints. Pour tempera paint on a large sponge in a Styrofoam meat tray. Slide the packaging material across the sponge. Carefully arrange the bubble wrap on construction paper to create interesting bubble prints.

2. RUBBINGS

Bring used copy paper and large crayons on a walk around the school grounds. Look for items to use in crayon rubbings, such as leaves, tree bark, concrete sidewalks, manhole covers, and so on. Place a piece of used paper over the item, printed-side down, and gently rub the crayon over the items to make imprints.

3. RAINBOW CRAYONS

Save old crayons that have been worn down. Have the children peel all the paper off the crayons. Then break the crayons into pieces about 1-inch long. Place all the pieces in a muffin tin. Bake in the oven at 200° until melted. Cool completely. The children will love these new crayons because they make lots of colors at one time.

4. SPONGE PAINT PAD

Place an old sponge in an aluminum pie tin or disposable plastic plate. Pour tempera paint on the sponge to make a paint pad for printing activities. A sponge can also be used to lightly paint surfaces, such as hands for handprints or feet for footprints.

5. STONE CREATURES

Paint smooth, medium-sized rocks with tempera paint. Decorate the rocks with glitter, wiggly eyes, fur pieces, buttons, pieces of yarn, and so on.

6. FALL OBJECT SORT

Collect a variety of acorns, chestnuts, walnuts, black walnuts, catalpa tree pods, and so on. Explain that each nut or pod is a seed for a tree. Glue each seed to a shoebox lid. Sort seeds by color, size, or shape.

Variation: Cut seeds in two and glue the halves on shoebox lids. Provide students with magnifying glasses to examine the seeds. Discuss the likenesses and differences of the seeds.

7. STARCH GHOSTS

Have an empty plastic dishwashing liquid bottle filled with water for each child. Take 10" x 10" pieces of cheesecloth and dip them into a liquid starch mixture (recipe listed here). Drape the cheesecloth over the bottles and let them dry completely. When dry, the starched cheesecloth is shaped like a ghost. Lift the ghosts from the bottles, and glue two black circles for the eyes on each. These make great table decorations for Halloween.

Liquid Starch Mixture

Use two parts glue to one part liquid starch. Pour starch into glue, a little at a time, and mix. Add more starch if needed so mixture is not sticky. Cover and chill overnight.

8. STONE PAPERWEIGHTS

Take students on a nature walk to collect medium-sized rocks with smooth surfaces. Decorate each rock using a variety of colors of tempera paint to make paperweights.

9. TOSS GAME

Cut off the top of a ½-gallon cardboard milk carton. Place a beanbag in the bottom of the carton so it won't tip over. Have the children toss Ping-Pong balls into the container from different distances. Have children count how many balls they can get in the container!

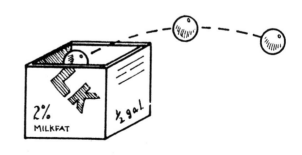

10. PIE TIN BIRDBATH

Glue an aluminum pie tin to a piece of plywood. Place the birdbath on the ground in an area that is easily visible from your classroom window. Fill the pie tin with water. Watch to see who uses the birdbath.

11. TWIG HOUSE

Collect ½-pint milk cartons. Cover the container with glue and small straight twigs and sticks to represent logs. To complete the twig house, cut out and glue on paper windows and doors.

Variation: For a challenge, cut out the doors and windows from the milk carton before gluing the twigs in place. The sticks will need to fit around the doors and windows.

12. PINECONE BIRD FEEDERS

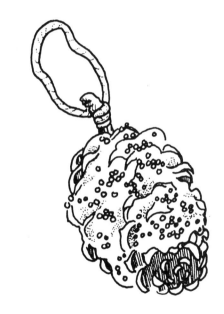

Collect large pinecones for this activity. Spread peanut butter with a tongue depressor over the pinecone and roll the pinecone in a 9" x 13" pan of birdseed. Attach a piece of string to the pinecone for hanging in a tree.

Variation: Bring an orange juice squeezer to school and make fresh orange juice. Cut the oranges in half and let the children squeeze the oranges using the machine. Let the orange rinds dry out until the next day. Then, make small holes in each side of the orange rinds. Thread string through the two holes in each rind and tie knots on the inside of the rinds for hanging from a tree. Then fill the orange-rind halves with birdseed or nuts. If possible, hang the bird feeders from a tree near a classroom window for the students to observe.

13. ACORN NECKLACES

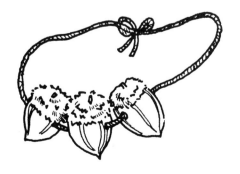

Save acorns in the fall. Have an adult volunteer drill a hole through each acorn for stringing. String the acorns to make bracelets and necklaces.

14. MESSAGE HOLDER

Paint empty metal band-aid containers with spray paint. When the paint dries, cut out designs or pictures from contact paper and attach to the containers. Place squares of blank paper and a pencil inside each container.

15. SNOWFLAKE ORNAMENT

For each snowflake ornament, glue eight popsicle sticks together diagonally on top of each other. Paint the popsicle sticks white. Then glue a paper clip to one end of the snowflake and hang from a tree.

16. DISPLAY TREE

Choose a three-to four-foot well-twigged branch. Place the branch in a large coffee can filled with plaster of paris. After the plaster has dried completely, paint the branches white. Set the branch in a corner of your room on the floor as a display for art projects celebrating the various seasons and holidays. Some suggestions might include:

Fall—paper apples, waxed leaves
Thanksgiving—clay fruit and vegetables hung on strings, pinecone turkeys
December—Christmas/Hanukkah decorations
Winter—snowflakes, snowballs, snowpeople
February—paper or doily hearts, hearts cut from clear plastic lids and decorated with markers
March—shamrocks
Spring—flowers, clay Easter eggs, pom-pom caterpillars, butterflies

17. POSTAGE STAMPS GIFTS

Laminate or cover canceled postage stamps with clear contact paper. Create earrings, pins, button covers, or barrettes with jewelry hardware from craft stores. Or, attach magnetic tape to the back of the stamps for refrigerator magnets. Canceled stamps can also be used for pictures in dollhouses or dioramas.

18. BAROMETER

For each barometer, you will need one small, wide-mouth jar, a large balloon, a rubberband, a drinking straw, and glue. Cut a piece of balloon large enough to cover the mouth of the jar when stretched. Secure the balloon in place with a rubberband. Glue one end of a drinking straw to the center of the balloon. Place the barometer next to a piece of cardboard about 12" long and at least 2" taller than the barometer. Fold the cardboard so it will stand behind the barometer. Pinch the end of the straw and mark the level of the straw on the cardboard each day with a different color of marker. At the end of the week, see how much the air pressure changed.

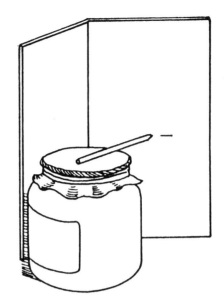

19. BEADS

Make beads from tapered strips of colored paper, such as old envelopes, advertising circulars, and so on. Cut paper ½" to 1" wide and approximately 6" to 8" long. Cut the paper diagonally to make two tapered strips. Starting at the wide end, dot glue down the length of the paper and roll tightly around a pencil. Place a small piece of tape on the paper to hold it until completely dry. Remove the paper bead from the pencil. Paint the beads with glue thinned with water to create a shiny surface. Use the beads for necklaces or bracelets.

Variation: Use beads to create sequence patterns. For example, two blue beads, three multi-colored beads, two blue beads, four multi-colored beads, two blue beads, and so on. Patterns can be simple or complex depending on the ability of the students.

Variation: Use beads to create 3-dimensional mosaics. This can be very effective with social studies concepts. Create backgrounds on construction paper with crayons, markers, or paper scraps. Sketch a large object in the centers of the pictures. Fill in the outlined shape with beads. Use ¼" to ½" wide untapered strips for the beads.

20. WATERMELONS

Make watermelon shapes out of construction paper. Glue real seeds to the watermelons to appear more realistic.

21. OLD SHOE PLANTER

Decorate old shoes with fabric paint, metallic paint, and glitter. Place potted plants in the openings of the shoes.

22. POSTAGE STAMP FLAGS

Collect canceled stamps from different parts of the world. Glue each stamp to a toothpick to make flags. Use small clay balls as flag stands. Place a map of the world on a table and arrange the flags on the different countries. Keep track during the year of which countries have flags.

23. LEATHER-LOOK VASES

Tear old paper lunch bags into irregular pieces, about the size of a half-dollar. Glue the pieces to small bottles and coffee cans. Smooth the edges, making sure all are securely glued in place. When dry, apply liquid brown shoe polish to the surface, creating a leather appearance. Decorate with permanent markers and use as vases.

24. FALL WINDOWS

Provide 8" x 10" pieces of clear contact paper, leaves in bright colors, and crayon shavings for this activity. If necessary, help children peel the backing off the contact paper. Arrange leaves on the contact paper and sprinkle with crayon shavings. Place another piece of contact paper on top of the leaves to seal the arrangements. Trim the edges. Paper punch a hole in the top of each of the arrangements, thread string through the holes, and display the arrangements in the window.

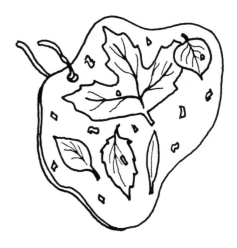

25. DISPLAY CASES

Tape around the edges of clean tuna fish cans. Arrange the cans in a shallow box and glue in place. Use the box for classifying, displaying collections, and observing small specimens. Include a magnifying glass for closer observation.

26. MILK CARTON PUPPETS

Cut the tops off quart or ½-gallon milk cartons and cover with construction paper. Glue tongue depressors approximately 2" inside the milk cartons as handles. Glue a picture of one of the characters in a story or book on each side of the milk cartons. Use the puppets to tell the stories from the characters' viewpoints. Encourage students to change characters.

Variation: Choose one character and add character traits to the other three sides of the milk carton, using words and pictures.

27. MINIATURE SHADOW BOXES

Tape around the edges of clean tuna fish cans. Create scenes or displays inside the cans, such as story settings, parts of flowers, or state symbols. Decorate the outsides of the cans with ribbon, lace, shells, contact paper, and so on. Glue strips of magnetic tape to the backs of the shadow boxes to create refrigerator displays.

28. MURAL

Read the poem "Sarah Cynthia Sylvia Stout Would Not Take the Garbage Out" by Shel Silverstein in *Where the Sidewalk Ends* (New York: Harper & Row, 1974). Design a mural with a big house. Take the students on a walk outside to find trash to add to the mural. Provide the students with plastic disposable gloves to use when collecting trash. Also, give students some guidelines as to what garbage will be appropriate to glue on the mural and what will not. Great discussions about littering and keeping our environment clean will occur as a result of this activity.

29. SEEDS

Save the seeds from plants each year to recycle and use for the next year. Share seeds with other teachers to increase the variety of plants. Experiment to find out which seeds are most hearty, bountiful, and fun to watch grow.

30. FANTASY VS. REALITY

Tape pieces of butcher paper to the wall. Divide the paper into two sections, one side labeled "Fantasy" and the other labeled "Reality." Invite children to cut out pictures from magazines and glue them to the appropriate sections of the paper.

31. PICTURE ORNAMENT

Cut strips approximately ¼" to ½" wide starting from the tops of paper kitchen or bathroom cups. Fold back the strips. Trim students' pictures to fit in the center of the bottom of the cups. Punch a hole in one of the top strips of each ornament and attach a paper clip through the holes. Tie yarn to the paper clips and hang the ornaments from the tree.

32. CLOUD PICTURES

Read the book *It Looked Like Spilt Milk* by Charles G. Shaw (New York: Harper & Row, 1947). Design clouds using glue, dryer lint, and dark blue paper. Then take the students outside to look at the cloud formations. Discuss the different types of clouds. (For more information about clouds, refer to these Fearon Teacher Aids titles *Weather Watch,* FE096, for primary grades, and *The Weather Report,* FE7511, for older grades. For a catalog, call 1-800-242-7272.)

 # PAPER BAGS

1. FEED THE ANIMALS

Stand a paper grocery bag upside down, so that the opening is on the bottom. Draw a picture of an animal head with its mouth wide open on the bottom of the paper bag. Cut out the mouth, leaving a hole big enough to throw scraps of paper into. Write the words "Please feed me trash" underneath the mouth. Place the paper bag animal over a trash can to encourage the students to throw away garbage and "feed" the animal.

2. GINGERBREAD PEOPLE

Cut gingerbread people out of brown grocery bags (see pattern on page 48). Decorate the gingerbread people with felt scraps, twist ties, sequins, yarn scraps, wiggly eyes, seeds, and tissue paper. Make gingerbread-people cookies for a snack using the following recipe.

Gingerbread People Recipe

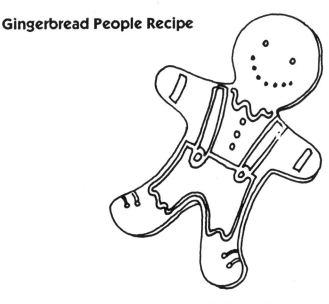

$\frac{1}{2}$ cup margarine
1 tsp cinnamon
1 cup sugar
2 tsp ginger
1 cup molasses
1 tsp salt
2 eggs
7 to 8 cups flour
1 tsp baking soda
$\frac{2}{3}$ cup water
1 tsp cloves

Cream together margarine and sugar; add eggs and molasses. Set aside. Sift together dry ingredients. Add to first mixture alternately with water. Add enough flour to make dough moldable and not sticky. Bake at 350° for about 8 minutes. This recipe makes 15 to 20 large gingerbread cookies.

Pattern for "Gingerbread People" (page 47)

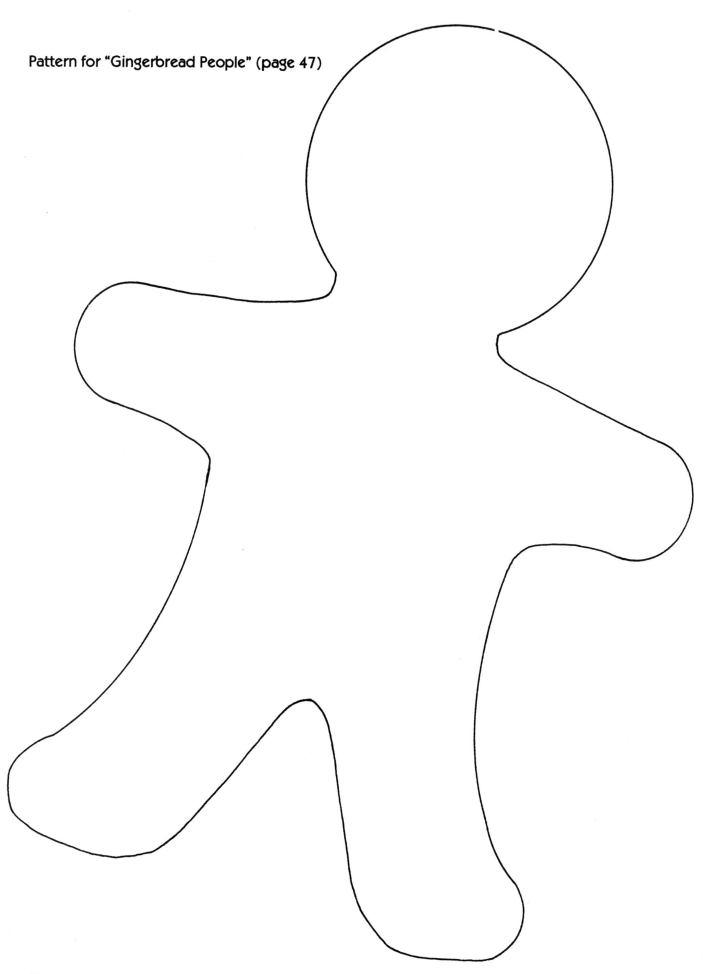

48

3. THINGS ABOUT ME WALL HANGING

Cut out the front or back section of a paper grocery bag. Fold one end over a dowel and glue. Tie a piece of yarn to each end of the dowel to display. Glue a picture of each student to the top of his or her own wall hanging. Have students copy fill-in-the-blank sentences on their wall hangings. Write the student's responses on the wall hangings, too. These make great displays for Open House!

Possible Fill-In Sentences:

1. My name is _____.
2. My family lives in _____.
3. My favorite place to go with my family is _____.
4. I like to eat _____.
5. I like to _____ at school.
6. Two words to describe me are _____ and _____.
7. I like to read books about _____.

4. TREASURE BAG

Decorate paper lunch bags with markers and stickers. Take a nature walk to collect treasures. Limit the number of natural treasures the students may collect to avoid disrupting the environment.

Variation: Use treasure bags for scavenger hunts. Give students specific lists of items to hunt for outdoors. This activity can be done individually or in groups.

5. VALENTINE'S DAY ACTIVITY

Make mail-delivery houses out of paper grocery bags. Stand the paper bags upright and cut the tops into triangle shapes to look like roofs. Decorate the paper-bag houses. Label each house with a student's name and street address. Have students bring a valentine for each student and deliver it to his or her paper bag house. Use mail carrier bags (see Mail Carrier Bags in this section) to deliver the valentines or other messages throughout the year.

6. ROLLED PAPER BEADS

Cut 1" x 4" rectangles out of paper bag material. Have children roll each rectangle over a 1-inch dowel and glue to form a rectangular bead. Children may want to make several beads. After they are thoroughly dry, the children can paint their beads. The next day they are ready to string into a necklace.

7. MAIL CARRIER BAGS

Fold down a 2-inch flap around the tops of large paper grocery bags and staple around the edges. Decorate the bags to look like mail bags. Staple fabric straps to the sides of the paper bags.

8. ROLLED-PAPER SCULPTURES

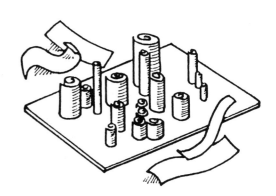

Cut paper bags into 2-inch, 4-inch, and 6-inch strips in various lengths. Create sculptures by rolling strips of paper into a variety of sizes of circles. Arrange the circles in a design on heavy matboard and glue in place. Allow the sculptures to dry thoroughly before decorating with fluorescent paint.

9. VEGETABLE PRINT WRAPPING PAPER

Provide a variety of different vegetables to use for printing. Cut paper grocery bags open and lay them flat. Place a sponge in an aluminum pie tin and cover with tempera paint. Choose the vegetables to be used and cut them in half. Press vegetable halves into the sponge and print the shapes on the paper to make decorative wrapping paper

10. SPORTS MURAL

Divide the class into small cooperative learning groups. Assign each group a sports theme to use when designing their murals, such as baseball, football, hockey, swimming, soccer, basketball, and so on. Provide each group with a large paper grocery bag, construction paper, scissors, glue, and markers. Cut open the grocery bags and use them as the backgrounds for each group's mural. Emphasize the importance of team work in completing this project.

11. CUBE SCULPTURE

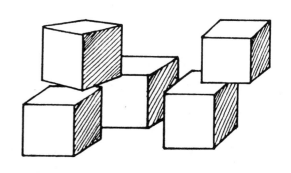

Cut out the cube (see pattern on page 52) using paper grocery bags. Have the children make several cubes by folding the pattern on the dotted lines and gluing the flaps together. Arrange the cubes into a design and glue on heavy matboard.

12. STORAGE CONTAINERS

Place one grocery bag inside of another and fold down a 2-inch flap and staple around the edges. Label each bag with the material to be stored inside.

13. PAPER BAG STUFFED BALLOONS

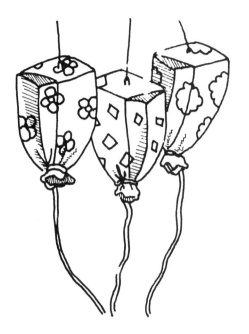

Stuff paper lunch bags with newspaper. Tie the open ends with yarn, leaving one long piece of yarn. Paint the bags in a variety of colors. Allow the bags to dry completely. Attach thread to paper clips and push the paper clips inside the tops of the bags. Then, attach another paper clip to the other end of the thread. Hang the balloons from the ceiling.

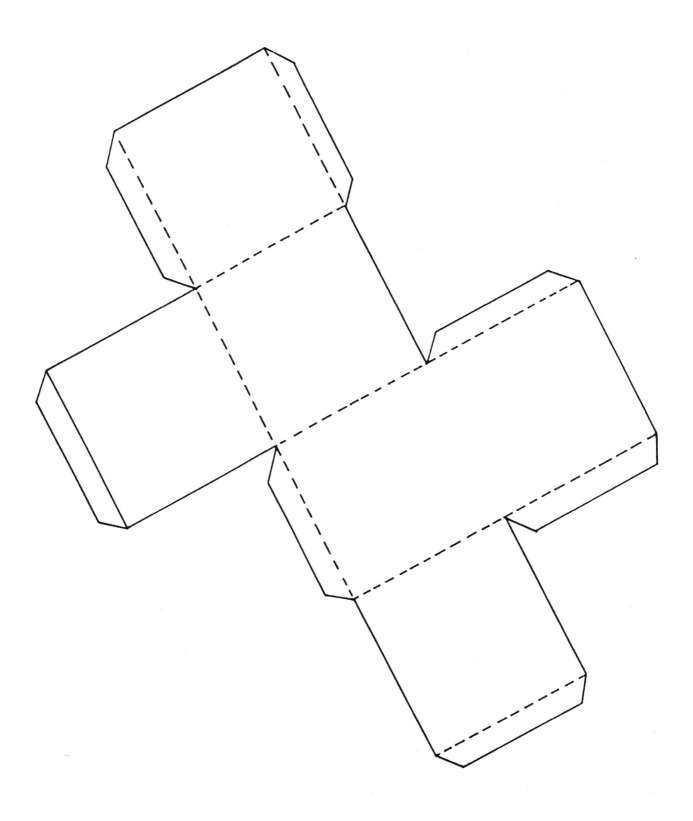

# Paper Tubes

1. NAPKIN RINGS

Use an X-acto knife to cut toilet-tissue tubes into 2-inch lengths. Cover the tubes with wallpaper, fabric, or felt. Add felt cut-outs of holly and berries for the winter holidays and flower and leaf cut-outs for Mother's or Father's Day gifts.

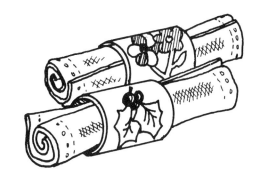

2. TUBE PEOPLE

Make tube people for the different seasons and holidays. For example, to make pilgrims, cover one toilet tissue tube with orange or brown paper. Cover another tube with black or gray paper. The tubes can also be painted these colors. Cut white collars and circles for faces (see patterns on page 54). Cut a white hat for the girl and a black or gray hat for the boy. Glue a yellow or gold buckle and band to the boy's hat (see patterns on page 54). Glue all the pieces in place. Tape the toilet tissue tubes to oaktag circles for greater stability.

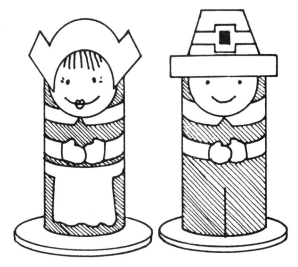

To make a snowperson, paint or cover a toilet tissue tube with white paper. Cut out a black top hat and white circle for the face (see patterns on page 54). Glue the pieces in place. Decorate with real buttons or draw buttons on with a marker.

3. MOUSE

Cut one third of a toilet tissue tube into a spiral. Leave the spiral attached to the tube as the mouse's tail. Cut a cone shape from gray construction paper for the mouse's face. Add features with markers and crayons. Glue the face to the front of the tube and add carpet thread for whiskers. Suggestion: Several books that can be used in conjunction with this project are *Whose Mouse Are You?* by Robert Kraus (New York: Macmillan, 1970) for young children and *Frederick* by Leo Leonni (New York: Knopf, 1967) for older children.

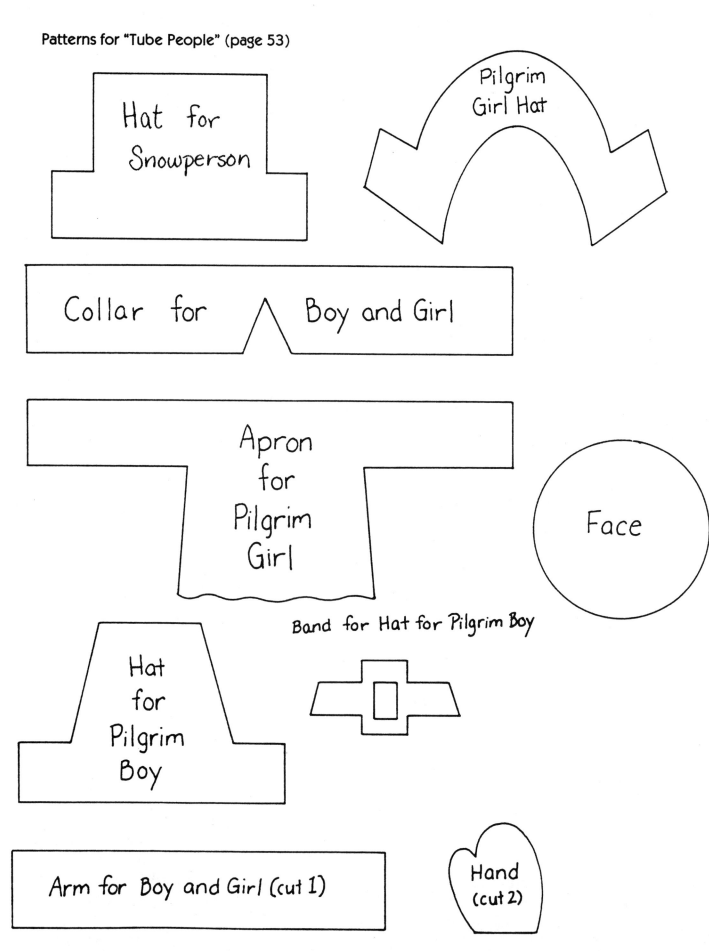

Hat for Snowperson

Pilgrim Girl Hat

Collar for Boy and Girl

Apron for Pilgrim Girl

Face

Band for Hat for Pilgrim Boy

Hat for Pilgrim Boy

Arm for Boy and Girl (cut 1)

Hand (cut 2)

4. TOTEM POLES

Take either toilet-tissue or paper-towel tubes and cover them with brown construction paper. Decorate individual circles to look like animal or bird heads and glue on the totem poles. Look at actual examples of Native American totem poles for design ideas.

5. HOLIDAY ORNAMENTS

To make spiral ornaments, cut a toilet-tissue tubes in half. Decorate the ornaments with tempera paint, markers, and glitter. Allow the paint to dry overnight. Carefully cut around the tubes to form spirals, then stretch them out slightly. Tie a string to one end of each ornament for hanging.

Variation: To make window ornaments, cut toilet-tissue tubes in half. Have an adult volunteer help the students cut out large diamonds in the sides of the tubes. Decorate the ornaments with tempera paint, markers, or glitter. Cut 2" x 5" pieces of colored cellophane. Paint around the diamond shapes on the insides of the tubes with glue. Place pieces of cellophane over the glue to make diamond-shaped windows. Attach string to hang each ornament.

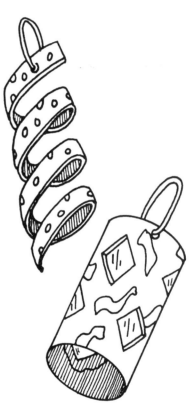

Variation: To make foil ornaments, cut toilet-tissue tubes in half. Use a hole punch to create holes in the sides of the tubes. Decorate the tubes with paint, markers, or glitter. Paint a thin layer of glue on the insides of the tubes. Place 2" x 5" pieces of aluminum foil or colored foil paper inside the tubes so that the shiny sides show through the holes. Tie string to one end of each ornament to display.

6. WINDSOCK

Construct animals, people, or creatures from large-width cardboard tubes, such as wrapping paper tubes. Cut the tubes in half. Decorate the tubes with stickers, markers, paint, and crepe-paper streamers and then hang the windsocks from the ceiling.

Plastic Berry Baskets

1. SPRING BASKETS

Weave ribbon, yarn or fabric strips through the ribbed sections of plastic berry baskets. Add pipe-cleaner handles and fill the baskets with shredded cellophane grass or newspaper strips. Younger students may prefer decorating paper panels and then gluing them to the sides of the baskets.

2. SORTING

Use baskets for sorting and classifying games. Draw pictures on paper panels of the items to be sorted into each basket. Glue the panels to the baskets. Then sort items by color, shape, size, or texture. Or, classify objects into categories, such as foods, animals, clothing, toys, and so on.

3. ANIMAL CAVES

Create cave openings by cutting holes in one side of berry baskets. Glue the baskets upside down to pieces of heavy cardboard. Cut lightweight muslin large enough to drape over each basket and onto the board. Place the muslin and fabric stiffener into a plastic zip-lock bag. Squeeze the bag to work the stiffener into the fabric. Drape the cloth over the baskets, leaving the cave entrances open. When the fabric is dry, paint the caves. Have students research and make clay models of animals that live in caves.

4. NESTING BASKETS

Fill berry baskets with "soft" materials birds might use to build their nests, such as yarn, fiberfill, cotton balls, dryer lint, and strands of frayed burlap. Tie string to the tops of the baskets and hang them in a tree. Pull a few strands through the basket mesh to help the birds get started.

5. STORAGE TRAYS

Use berry baskets to keep art supplies organized, such as scissors, paintbrushes, crayons, and so on. Also store pieces of chalk, extra pencils, game pieces, counters, and so on in easily accessible baskets. The baskets can be labeled with paper panels explaining the contents.

6. PRINTING

Set up several sponge pads with various colors of tempera paint. Press the basket bottoms into the sponges and press firmly onto paper to produce an interesting "waffle" effect.

7. BUBBLE MAKERS

Make a soapy solution for students to enjoy outside or at home. Experiment with blowing bubbles through the bottom of the baskets.

8. MOBILES

Choose a theme for mobiles, such as transportation or the environment. Draw or cut out pictures from magazines that correspond to the theme. Punch holes in the tops of pictures and tie to a variety of lengths of yarn. Hang the pictures from the side panels of the berry baskets. Thread string or yarn through the bottoms of the baskets and turn the mobiles upside down. Hang the mobiles from the ceiling.

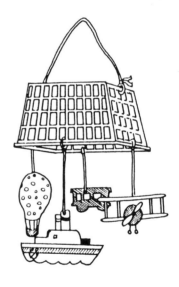

 # Plastic Containers

1. NATURE IMPRINTS

Pour plaster of paris into the plastic lids of coffee cans. Provide a variety of seeds, leaves, rocks, sticks, flowers, and so on to be imprinted in the plaster. After the plaster circles are completely dry, remove the coffee can lids.

Variation: Use other sizes of plastic lids to make nature imprints.

2. BASKET WEAVING

Take large Cool Whip containers and cut slits about one inch apart down the sides of the containers. Caution the children to be careful of any sharp plastic edges. Have the children weave the sides together using 1/4-inch reeds, construction-paper strips, or ribbon.

3. SAND LAYERING

Use clear yogurt or salad containers with lids. Have different colored sand available for the children to use. Experiment with layering different colors of sand in the clear containers.

4. NESTS

Save dry grass clippings. Fill margarine tubs with grass clippings, small pieces of leaves, moss, yarn, dryer lint, and so on. Pack the nesting materials against the insides of the tubs to create bowl-shaped nests. Make small eggs from clay or playdough. Allow the eggs to dry completely, then paint the eggs. Carefully set the painted eggs in the nests. Place the lids on the margarine tubs to carry the nests home.

5. PLANET MURAL

Collect a variety of sizes and colors of plastic lids. Choose nine lids to represent the planets of the solar system. Glue the lids to a piece of blue or black butcher paper.

6. PARTS OF A CELL

Create a model of a cell using a margarine lid. Label the cell membrane and the cytoplasm. For the nucleus, crumple up a small piece of scrap paper and glue in the center of the lid. Cells can be made more complex, depending on the ability level of students.

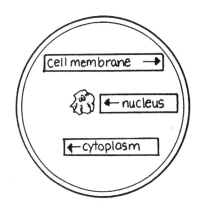

7. VISOR

Cut large, soft plastic lids in half-moon shapes. Make ½-inch slits along the inner rims. Fold back the slits and cover the edges with masking or fabric tape. Punch a hole on each side of the outer edges of the lids. Tie rubberbands together to make stretchy bands to fit each students' head. Decorate the visors with permanent markers.

8. SYNONYMS, ANTONYMS, AND ANALOGIES

Find magazine or supermarket flyer pictures that show pairs of synonyms, antonyms, or analogies, such as mustard is to hot dogs as milk is to cereal. Use margarine lids as guides for cutting out pictures. Glue the pictures inside the margarine lids.

9. GREATER THAN, LESS THAN

Cut a wedge shape out of a margarine lid and use a permanent marker to make a character similar to Pacman. Explain to students that the character always eats the larger amount. Each child can make his or her own character to help learn the concept of greater than or less than.

10. LEAF SORT

Collect fall leaves from a variety of trees and bushes. Glue one of each variety of leaf on clear, plastic margarine lids or lids from salad bar containers. Sort the leaves by color, size, or shape. Punch a hole in each lid, tie a piece of fishing line to the lids, and hang the lids in the window.

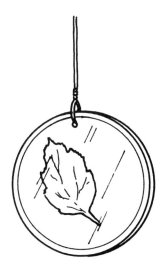

11. SPIDERS

Use small Cool Whip or margarine containers. Turn the containers upside down. Paper punch eight holes in the sides of each container and attach pipe cleaners for the legs. Glue a pair of wiggly eyes to the front of each container. To make the spiders walk, carefully puncture two holes in the tops of the spiders. Tie one end of a piece of yarn to each container and the other end to a chopstick or dowel.

12. SHAPE GAME

Use a large Cool Whip container with a lid for this game. Cut four shapes out of the lid, and put the lid back on the container. Cut the same sized shapes out of sponges. Let the children match the shapes. The container is great for storing the sponge shapes, too.

13. TERRARIUMS

Go on a nature walk to collect rocks, moss, tiny ferns, small plants, and so on. Fill the bottom of clear, plastic salad-bar containers with soil. Arrange the plants and the rocks in the bottom of the terrariums. Encourage interested students to add plastic figurines, too. Water the plants and snap the lids on tightly. The terrariums should be self-sustaining for a period of time. When the soil feels dry, open the lids and add water.

14. AQUARIUMS

Create an aquarium using clear, plastic lids from salad-bar containers. Provide materials to make seashells, sandpaper starfish, and metallic-paper fish. Add tinsel, colored sand, glitter, and other details to make the aquatic designs more interesting. Encourage the students to experiment with different ways of gluing the aquarium inhabitants on the plastic lids.

15. SAND DESIGNS

Use clear, plastic salad-bar container lids for this activity. Make designs with glue (small glue bottles work the best) on the plastic lids. Then sprinkle different colors of sand over the glue designs. Provide containers to shake off the excess sand.

16. FOSSILS

Pour ½" of wet sand in the bottoms of margarine tubs. Press stones, shells, leaves, twigs and acorns into the sand to create impressions. Carefully remove the objects. Pour one inch of plaster of paris mixed with water into the margarine tubs. Allow to harden completely. Carefully remove the plaster from the containers.

Variation: Create paperweights by placing a layer of dry sand in the bottoms of the margarine tubs. Place the items on top of the sand. Then carefully pour the plaster over the objects. Remove the plaster when hardened. The objects should be imbedded in the sandy surface.

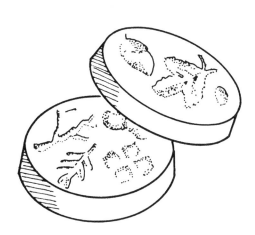

17. GRASS HUTS

Turn margarine tubs upside down and carefully cut a door shape in the side of each tub. Collect dried grass clippings. Cover the tubs with Elmer's glue and press dried grass onto the surfaces. Allow the glue to dry completely before moving the huts. Place the huts on large cardboard bases to create villages. Add other details to the villages, such as animals, trees, and so on. Research to find out more information about the countries where grass huts may be used as houses.

18. LIQUID CAPACITY

Collect a variety of sizes of clean liquid containers. The labels should be left on the containers. Sort containers according to milliliters, liters, ounces, quarts, pints, and gallons. Place each container in the category representing the largest unit of measurement.

19. TEPEES

Provide each student with a small Cool Whip lid, a paper lunch bag, six popsicle sticks, masking tape, yarn, crayons, scissors, and a container of water. Place the lids upside down on the table. Tape the popsicle sticks vertically along the outside edges of the lids. Carefully lean the sticks to the center. Have an adult volunteer or another student help tie yarn around the sticks to hold them in place. Then cut the paper bags open so they lay flat. Before decorating the tepees, have students research which Native American tribes actually lived in tepees, how they were built, why they were used, and the significance of the designs on the outside walls. Decorate the outside of the paper bags. Then carefully immerse the bags in water. Gently unfold the paper bags and wrap them around the popsicle stick frameworks. Allow the tepees to dry overnight.

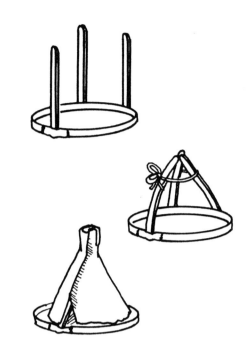

20. MANIPULATIVE ACTIVITY

Puncture sixteen holes in the lid of a large Cool Whip container. Trace around the inside of the lid to create several paper disks. On each paper disk mark the locations of the sixteen holes on the Cool Whip lid. Create several different designs using crayons to mark the holes. Place the lid back on the Cool Whip container. Choose a paper-circle design for the top of the lid. Have children match different colored golf tees to the designs on the lid. The Cool Whip container is great for storing the circles and pegs, too.

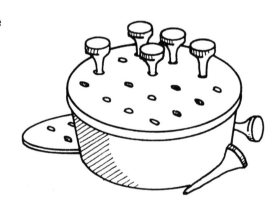

21. UNDERWATER VIEWING SCOPE

Use the bottom of a clear, plastic salad-bar container as a viewing scope. Arrange several seashells and other treasures on the bottom of a plastic tub of water. For added effect, add a few drops of blue food coloring to the water. Place the viewing scope on the surface of the water. Look at the objects on the bottom of the tub with the viewing scope. Use this activity as a motivator for writing underwater adventure stories.

22. INSECT OBSERVATORY

Take a clear, plastic salad-bar container with a lid and punch several air holes in the top. Arrange grass, leaves, and twigs to create a habitable environment for insects. Observe the specimens for a short time and then release.

23. PAIL PLANTER

Decorate ice-cream pails with stickers and colored contact paper. Place a layer of rocks in the bottoms of the pails for drainage. Fill the containers with potting soil. Plant a tree sapling or several small hearty houseplants in each pail. When the saplings are large enough, plant them outside for all to enjoy.

Plastic Jar Lids

Jar lids from peanut butter, instant coffee, iced tea, or powdered non-dairy creamer would be appropriate for the following activities.

1. COLLECTOR'S PAPERWEIGHT

Fill large jar lids with plaster of paris. (You can leave them white or tint with food coloring.) When the plaster begins to harden, carefully arrange items in the jar lids, such as seashells, buttons, beads, dried beans, and so on. Allow the paperweights to dry overnight. If desired, decorate the outside rims with ribbon, rickrack, vinyl tape, or sewing trim.

2. NUMBER SEQUENCE GAME

Use a permanent marker to mark the tops of lids with numbers in sequences, such as twos, fives, tens, and so on. Have students arrange the lids in the correct numerical sequence. Mark the insides of the lids with other sequences.

3. MATH SORT

Number a set of lids from one to fifteen. Provide a number of small items to place in the lids, such pebbles, metal washers, or uncooked rotini noodles—one item in lid #1, 2 items in lid #2, and so on. Encourage students to practice arranging the counters in different patterns.

4. CIRCLE MATCH

Write color words on a variety of different-sized lids—red, orange, yellow, green, blue, purple, pink, white, brown, and black. Create a game board by tracing the various sizes of lids and filling in the circles with the colors listed above. Encourage children to match the color words written on the lids with the appropriate circles on the game board.

5. MATH MATCH

Using the numbered lids prepared in the Math Sort activity, prepare a matching set of lids containing the corresponding number of items glued in place so that, for example, lid #1 matches up with a lid that has one item glued inside it. Challenge students to practice recognizing the numbers of items by sight rather than counting.

6. SHOEBOX VEHICLES

Turn shoeboxes upside down and paint or cover them with contact paper. Provide a variety of sizes of jar lids to use as tires, headlights, and taillights. For windows, use mirror paper or regular construction paper. Add passengers to the shoebox vehicles before gluing windows in place.

7. PHOTO MAGNET

Ask students to bring in a photograph of themselves. Place the lids on top of the pictures and carefully trace around them with a pencil or pen. Trim the photos to fit inside the plastic jar lids. Glue magnets on the backs of the lids. Decorate the outside of the lids with ribbon, pasta shapes, lace, and so on.

8. SHAKERS

Provide two of the same size peanut-butter jar lids and a "noisy" material, such as rice, dried beans, jingle bells, or unpopped popcorn. Place several dried beans inside one of the lids. Rubber cement the edges of the two lids together. Allow the glue to dry overnight. Shake the lids.

9. GERMINATION TRAYS

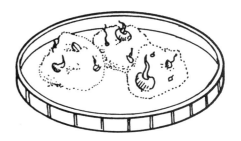

Spread out three or four cotton balls inside large plastic lids. Wet the cotton balls with water, then sprinkle with a few radish or bean seeds. Cover the lids with clear plastic wrap. Once the sprouts appear, plant the seeds in soil and watch them grow!

10. TEXTURE MATCH

Make several sets of lids with matching circles of textured material, such as velvet, corduroy, sandpaper, sponge, fur, or corrugated cardboard glued inside. Challenge students to match the sets of textured lids while blindfolded.

11. NATURE COLLAGES

Trace around large plastic lids on pieces of fabric. Cut the fabric circles to fit inside the lids. Take the students on a nature walk to find items to include in their collages, such as acorns, tiny pinecones, small leaves, dried corn, flowers, and weeds. Arrange the items inside the lids and glue the pieces in place.

12. HAND HELD MIRROR

Trace around large plastic lids on mirror paper. Cut out the circles and glue the circles inside the lids. Turn the lids over and glue large tongue depressors to the backs of the lids as handles. Allow the glue to dry. Trace and cut out circles of paper to glue to the backs of the mirrors. Decorate the paper circles with markers, sequins, stickers, and so on.

Variation: For a Mother's Day Gift, copy the following poem onto the backs of the mirrors:

> *Mirror, Mirror*
> *On the wall*
> *Who's the sweetest*
> *Mom of all?*
> *Turn over!*

Decorate the edges of these special gifts with ribbon, lace, small fabric flowers, and so on.

13. CONCENTRATION GAME

Create matching pairs of lids with identical pictures glued inside. Turn all the lids over with the picture-sides down. Have children take turns turning over two lids at a time, looking for matching pictures. The player with the most matches at the end of the game wins.

SUPERMARKET FLYERS

1. THANKSGIVING DINNER

Use supermarket flyers to put together a
Thanksgiving dinner. Make a list of the
foods that are often included at Thanksgiving, as well as foods the students would like
to include. Cut out large platters from wallpaper. Have the students cut out pictures of
foods for the Thanksgiving dinner from
supermarket flyers and magazines. Arrange
the pictures on the wallpaper platters and
glue in place. Have the students write or
dictate stories about the meal and attach to
the pictures.

2. GROCERY STORE DESIGN

Give each child a 12" x 18" piece of poster paper and glue. On the chalkboard, list
all the areas in a grocery store, such as produce, paper products, canned goods,
meat department, dairy department, bakery, and frozen foods. Have students
design the inside of a grocery store using cardboard pieces, construction-paper
scraps, markers, and supermarket flyers.

3. HUNGRY CREATURES

Read the story *The Hungry Thing* by Jan Slepian and Ann Seidler (Chicago:
Follett Publishing Co., 1967). Make hungry creatures out of large pieces of wallpaper, small fur pieces, and add wiggly eyes. Cut out pictures from supermarket
flyers to show foods that the Hungry Thing likes to eat. Glue the food pictures
around the Hungry Thing. Encourage students to come up with their own stories
and rhymes.

4. FOOD COLOR BOOKLET

Have your class work together to make a food
color booklet. Categorize and glue pictures of
food into the booklet by color. Write the color
word on each page.

5. CATERPILLAR FOOD

Read the story *The Very Hungry Caterpillar* by Eric Carle (New York: Putnam, 1983). Have the students look for the food items mentioned in the story in supermarket flyers. Encourage students to think of other foods that the caterpillar might like to eat, too.

6. FOOD GROUPS

Take a large piece of posterboard and separate it into six sections to follow the USDA's Food Guide Pyramid. (For an example of the pyramid, refer to American Teaching Aids' chart ATA 2165 *The Nutrition Pyramid.* For a catalog, call 1-800-423-6537.) Use supermarket flyers to cut out and glue pictures of foods for the different sections of the chart.

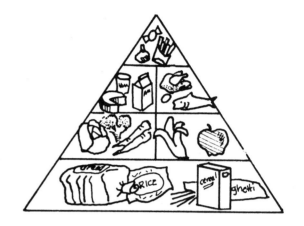

7. FOOD COLLAGE

Give students 12" x 18" pieces of construction paper, supermarket flyers, and magazines. Have students cut out all shapes and sizes of food pictures. Encourage the students to cover every inch of the construction paper with pictures. Display the food collages.

8. SHADOW MATCHING GAME

Use supermarket flyers to find six large pictures of food items. Trace around the pictures on a 8" x 10" piece of posterboard to create a game board with the food silhouettes. Color in the silhouettes with black marker or crayon. Laminate or cover the game board and food pictures with clear contact paper for durability. Match the food pictures with the correct shadows.

9. SUPERMARKET SHOPPING

Cut out pictures and prices of different foods from a variety of supermarket flyers. Glue the pictures to recipe cards and display around the room. Give each student $5.00 in play money. Have students write down the items they would like to buy on a shopping list. Remind the students that they only have $5.00 to spend.

10. THE PRICE IS RIGHT

Cut out pictures and prices of grocery store items from different supermarket flyers. Glue the pictures of the items on the front of 3" x 5" cards and the prices on the back. Have students estimate the cost of each product. Compare the students' guesses with the actual prices.

11. SHOPPING LIST

Have each student write out a shopping list for his or her family for one week. Have students make guesses as to the total cost of the items on their grocery lists. Then provide a variety of supermarket flyers for the students to use to find out the cost of as many items as possible on their lists. Add up the cost of the items on the grocery lists. Compare the guesses to the actual totals.

 # WALLPAPER

1. PHOTO HOUSE

Ask parents to send family pictures to school for a classroom collage. Use a shoebox lid to represent each student's house or apartment building. Cut out a triangular shape from wallpaper and glue it to the shoebox lid for a roof. Have each student cut and glue his or her family pictures inside the appropriate house or apartment building. On a large sheet of butcher paper, draw a map of a neighborhood. Tape the students' houses and apartment buildings on the map. Add other details, such as a library, school, grocery store, trees, flowers, and so on. Encourage students to share the pictures of their families with the rest of the class.

2. BULLETIN BOARD

Send a letter home to parents asking them to send a picture of their child to school. Cut a large school bus out of yellow butcher paper and staple it onto a bulletin board. Cut two wheels out of textured wallpaper and staple on the bus. Use 3" x 5" squares of wallpaper as bus windows. Staple the students' photographs to the bus windows.

3. FISHING GAME

Cut out fifteen wallpaper fish (see the pattern on page 72). Cover each fish with clear contact paper or laminating film for durability. Then attach a paper clip to each fish. Fishing poles are made by tying yarn to a small magnet and attaching a chopstick or dowel to the other end. Use a grease pencil to label the fish, using words with the same vowel sounds, matching parts of speech, finding synonyms, and so on.

Variation: Have students fish for characters or events from stories, answers to math problems, and so on.

4. SCALY PICTURES

Draw and cut out a large dinosaur from sheets of newspaper. Tape the pieces of the dinosaur together and set aside for later. Give each student an old file folder and a variety of 2" x 2" wallpaper squares. Glue the squares in rows across the file folder, starting at the bottom, and overlapping each row. Then arrange all the wallpaper file folders so they completely cover the newspaper dinosaur shape. The small wallpaper squares should create a scaly-looking dinosaur. Carefully trim the file folders to fit the dinosaur shape. Cover the wallpaper pieces with tempera paint. Allow the dinosaur to dry overnight. Add other details, such as eyes, teeth, and claws. When the dinosaur is finished, carefully tape it to a classroom wall.

Variations: Give each student a file folder to make his or her own dinosaur. Draw and cut out dinosaur shapes from the file folders. Cut the wallpaper pieces into 1" x 1" squares. Glue the pieces in rows starting at the bottom. Carefully trim around the dinosaur shapes. If interested, paint the dinosaurs with tempera paint.

5. COMMUNITY HELPER MURAL

Take a field trip to visit the community helpers in your area. Explain the jobs the community helpers do and the buildings where they work. As a follow-up activity, have the students create a mural showing the buildings in the community. Give the students a variety of square and rectangular wallpaper pieces to use as buildings. Glue the shapes to a large piece of butcher paper. Use popsicle sticks, buttons, yarn pieces, cardboard egg carton sections, markers, and matboard scraps to decorate the buildings. Decorate wooden ice-cream spoons to look like community helpers and glue to the mural, too.

6. FLOWER CENTERPIECES

Cut out flower patterns from old wallpaper books. Glue the flower shapes to popsicle sticks. Give each student a piece of Styrofoam packing or a lid of a Styrofoam egg carton to use as the base of their flower centerpieces. Stick the popsicle stick flowers in the Styrofoam. Decorate the bases with tempera paint, glitter, ribbon, rickrack, buttons, construction paper, and so on. Use the centerpieces as decorations for a spring party or as special gifts.

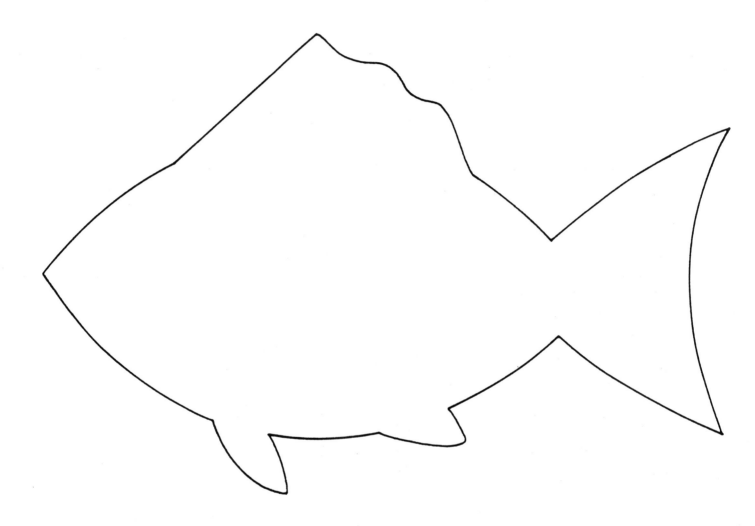

7. WALLPAPER CLOWNS

Design clowns using a variety of wallpaper pieces, construction paper, crayons, pom-poms, buttons, yarn, and glue. Fold the bodies of the clowns into accordion pleats to make them dance.

8. TEXTURE COLLAGE

Use a variety of textured pieces of wallpaper to create texture collages. Lay a piece of used copy paper over the different wallpaper samples and gently rub a crayon across each texture.

9. EGG TREE

In the spring, find a branch from an apple tree or lilac bush with lots of buds. Bring the branch back to the classroom and put it in a jar of water. Watch for the growth of leaves and possibly even blossoms. Cut out egg shapes from wallpaper patterns. Paper punch a hole in the top of each egg shape, and attach a piece of yarn. Find special spots on the tree to hang the eggs.

10. BODY TRACING

Visit the local newspaper printer to pick up ends of newsprint rolls and other paper scraps they would like to donate. Have each student lie down on the newsprint and have a partner trace around his or her body. Decorate the body shapes using crayons, markers, ribbon, trim, yarn, and wallpaper pieces for clothing and other details.

Dear Parents, Please Save for Me . . .

Aluminum pie tins

Aluminum TV-dinner trays

Beads

Boxes: oatmeal, shoeboxes, cigar, diaper, Band-Aid, storage (any size)

Burlap

Buttons

Calendars

Canvas

Cardboard soda cases (12-& 24-packs)

Cartons

Catalogs

Clothespins

Computer paper

Contact paper

Cornhusks

Costume jewelry

Crayon pieces

Deodorant bottles

Detergent bottles

Egg cartons (cardboard and Styrofoam)

Eggshells

Fabric scraps

File folders

Film containers, 35-mm

Gift-wrapping paper

Greeting cards

Junk mail

Keys

Magazines

Microwave dinner containers

Milk cartons—plastic, paper

Newspapers

Paper bags (all sizes)

Pinecones

Pizza boxes

Plastic berry baskets

Plastic bottles (all sizes)

Plastic containers (all sizes)

Plastic disposable plates

Plastic frozen juice cans and lids

Plastic salad-bar containers

Plastic silverware

Plastic six-pack holders

Ribbon

Seashells

Sheets

Sponges

Spools

Styrofoam containers

Supermarket flyers

Tissue paper

Trim scraps

Toothbrushes (for painting)

Wallpaper books

Wood scraps

Yarn

Beautiful Junk II © 1993 Fearon Teacher Aids

 # Materials for Collages and Constructions

Create wonderful projects from recyclable materials. Show your students that by reusing items, you are not only reducing landfill waste, but conserving energy and natural resources, too. Use this revised list as a starting point, then let your imagination be your guide as you build a wonderful collection of reusable materials for your classroom.

Aluminum foil

Aluminum pie tins

Bark

Beads: wood, plastic

Beans (dried)

Belts: buckles and leather straps

Birdseed

Blotter paper

Bobby pins and hair clips

Bottles and bottle caps (plastic, glass)

Boxes and cartons (variety of sizes and shapes)

Braid, rickrack, and trim

Bubble packaging material

Butcher paper

Buttons (all sizes)

Calendars

Candles

Cardboard scraps

Cards: holiday greeting cards, postcards

Carpet scraps

Catalogs: department store, mail order, seed and bulb

Chains

Clock parts

Coffee grounds

Contact paper (opaque and clear)

Corks

Cornhusks and kernels

Costume jewelry parts

Cotton balls

Dowels

Drapery and upholstery samples

Dried flowers, grasses, and seeds

Driftwood

Easter grass

Egg cartons: paper and Styrofoam

Eggshells (cleaned)

Elastic

Erasers

Fabric scraps: burlap, felt, oilcloth, silk, cotton, velvet, wool, vinyl

Feathers

Film canisters, 35-mm

Floor tile and linoleum scraps

Florist's supplies: foam, foil, ribbon, tape, and wire

Flowers: artificial and dried

Food trays: Styrofoam, clear plastic, and paper

Fur scraps

Game pieces: checkers, dice, dominoes

Glitter

Golf tees

Gravel

Ice-cream pails (plastic)

Inner-tube scraps

Junk mail

Key rings and tags

Keys

Lace

Leaves

Lids: jar, spray can, margarine
  containers, and so on

Magazines

Marbles

Masonite

Matboard scraps

Mosaic tile

Moss (dried)

Nails

Newspaper

Nuts and bolts

Nuts and nutshells

Paper confetti from paper punches

Paper bags (all sizes)

Paper scraps: construction paper, crepe
  paper, tissue paper

Paper tubes from household goods,
  mailing tubes

Pasta (dry)

Peanut butter

Pinecones

Pine needles

Ping-Pong balls

Pits: apricot, cherry, peach

Pizza boxes (cardboard)

Popsicle sticks

Ribbon scraps

Rice (uncooked)

Rope scraps

Rubberbands

Salad bar containers (clear, plastic)

Sand

Sandpaper

Sawdust

Screen

Screws

Seashells

Seedpods

Seeds: acorns, apple, orange, pumpkin,
  watermelon

Sewing tape: bias tape, seam binding

Shoelaces

Soap

Sponges

Spools of thread

Stamps (canceled)

Sticks and twigs

Stones and pebbles

String, twine, and cord

Styrofoam chips, packing materials, and
  trays

Supermarket flyers

Thread

Toothbrushes (old)

Wallpaper books

Wallpaper samples

Washers

Wire: copper, jewelry, telephone

Wood scraps and shavings

Wheels from toys

Wrapping paper and ribbon

Yarn

Zippers

Index of Activities

Classroom Equipment and Supplies

All About Me Supply Boxes (Boxes, 4)

Badges (Frozen Juice Can Lids, 1)

Base for Creations (Heavy Cardboard, 8)

Big Book (Newspaper, 11)

Book and Paper Holder (Boxes, 5)

Bookends (Boxes, 6)

Bulletin Board (Wallpaper, 2)

Chalkboard Stencils (Heavy Cardboard, 9)

Display Cases (Miscellaneous, 25)

Display Tree (Miscellaneous, 16)

Feed the Animals (Paper Bags, 1)

Floor Squares (Newspaper, 10)

Food Color Booklet (Supermarket Flyers, 4)

Food Groups (Supermarket Flyers, 6)

Geometry (Boxes, 8)

Germination Trays (Plastic Jar Lids, 9)

Greater Than, Less Than (Plastic Containers, 9)

Liquid Capacity (Plastic Containers, 18)

Manipulative Multiplication (Egg Cartons, 10)

Miniature Shadow Boxes (Miscellaneous, 27)

Playdough Cutter (Detergent Caps, 5)

Privacy Screens (Boxes, 2)

Recyclable Art Center (Boxes, 1)

Report Displays (Boxes, 3)

Sponge Paint Pad (Miscellaneous, 4)

Stamper (Frozen Juice Can Lids, 9)

Stencil Painting (Newspaper, 7)

Storage Containers (Paper Bags, 12)

Storage Trays (Plastic Berry Baskets, 5)

Synonyms, Antonyms, and Analogies (Plastic Containers, 8)

Treasure Bag (Paper Bags, 4)

Underwater Viewing Scope (Plastic Containers, 21)

Dramatic-Play Props

Binoculars (Egg Cartons, 4)

Crown (Egg Cartons, 7)

Mail Carrier Bags (Paper Bags, 7)

Milk Carton Characters (Miscellaneous, 26)

Shopping List (Supermarket Flyers, 11)

Supermarket Shopping (Supermarket Flyers, 9)

Traffic Lights (Frozen Juice Can Lids, 3)

Games

Circle Match (Plastic Jar Lids, 4)

Color Sorting (Film Canisters, 3)

Concentration Game (Plastic Jar Lids, 13)

Fabric Dominoes (Fabric, 7)

Fall Object Sort (Miscellaneous, 6)

Fishing Game (Wallpaper, 3)

Leaf Sort (Plastic Containers, 10)

Manipulative Activity (Plastic Containers, 20)

Math Match (Plastic Jar Lids, 5)

Math Sort (Plastic Jar Lids, 3)

Number Sequence Game (Plastic Jar Lids, 2)

Seriation Activities (Film Canisters, 7)

Shadow Matching Game (Supermarket Flyers, 8)

Shape Game (Plastic Containers, 12)

Six Food Groups (Boxes, 10)

Sniffers (Film Canisters, 1)

Sorting (Plastic Berry Baskets, 2)

Sound Match (Film Canisters, 2)

Texture Match (Plastic Jar Lids, 10)

The Price Is Right (Supermarket Flyers, 10)

Toss Game (Miscellaneous, 9)

Gift Ideas

Candle Holder (Detergent Caps, 4)

Coasters (Frozen Juice Can Lids, 2)

Collector's Paperweight (Plastic Jar Lid, 1)

Floral Bouquet (Detergent Caps, 1)

Flower Centerpieces (Wallpaper, 6)

Hand Held Mirror (Plastic Jar Lid, 12)

Hand Painted Wrapping Paper (Newspaper, 9)

Magnets (Frozen Juice Can Lids, 6)

Napkin Rings (Paper Tubes, 1)

Necklaces (Frozen Juice Can Lids, 8)

Newspaper Wrapping Paper (Newspaper, 12)

Paperweights (Frozen Juice Can Lids, 5)

Photo Magnet (Plastic Jar Lid, 7)

Photo Pins (Frozen Juice Can Lids, 4)

Planter (Detergent Caps, 6)

Postage Stamp Gifts (Miscellaneous, 17)

Recipe Card Holder (Detergent Caps, 2)

Stone Paperweights (Miscellaneous, 8)

Vegetable Print Wrapping Paper (Paper Bags, 9)

Holiday Projects

Balloon Ornament (Newspaper, 3)

Bean Wreath (Heavy Cardboard, 12)

Egg Tree (Wallpaper, 9)

Holiday Candle (Detergent Caps, 9)

Holiday Ornaments (Paper Tubes, 5)

Holiday Wreath (Egg Cartons, 1)

Picture Ornament (Miscellaneous, 31)

Santa (Egg Cartons, 12)

Snowflake Ornament (Miscellaneous, 15)

Special Cards (Fabric, 3)

Thanksgiving Dinner (Supermarket Flyers, 1)

Valentine's Day Activity (Paper Bags, 5)

Musical Instruments

Rattles (Film Canisters, 4)

Rhythm Instruments (Frozen Juice Can Lids, 10)

Shakers (Plastic Jar Lids, 8)

Wind Chimes (Frozen Juice Can Lids, 7)

Reading Activities

Caterpillar Food (Supermarket Flyers, 5)

Cloud Pictures (Miscellaneous, 32)

Corduroy Bears (Fabric, 2)

Hungry Creatures (Wallpaper, 3)

Monkey Puppets (Heavy Cardboard, 1)

Mouse Paint (Detergent Caps, 7)

Science Experiments

Barometer (Miscellaneous, 18)

Color Mixing (Film Canisters, 6)

Insect Observatory (Plastic Containers, 22)

Parts of a Cell (Plastic Containers, 6)

Rain Gauge (Film Canisters, 8)

Seeds (Miscellaneous, 29)

Student Art and Craft Projects

Acorn Necklaces (Miscellaneous, 13)

Animal Caves (Plastic Berry Baskets, 3)

Aquariums (Plastic Containers, 14)

Banner (Fabric, 12)

Basket Weaving (Plastic Containers, 2)

Beads (Miscellaneous, 19)

Body Tracing (Wallpaper, 10)

Braiding (Fabric, 8)

Bubble Blowers (Detergent Caps, 8)

Bubble Makers (Plastic Berry Baskets, 7)

Bubble Prints (Miscellaneous, 1)

Caterpillar (Egg Cartons, 5)

Character Hats (Fabric, 13)

Circle Printing (Detergent Caps, 3)

Class Quilt (Fabric, 10)

Clock (Egg Cartons, 2)

Community Helper Mural (Wallpaper, 5)

Creature Features (Egg Cartons, 3)

Cube Sculpture (Paper Bags, 11)

Egg Carton Bird Feeder (Egg Cartons, 9)

Egg Carton Sculptures (Egg Cartons, 6)

Fall Windows (Miscellaneous, 24)

Fantasy vs. Reality (Miscellaneous, 30)

Food Collage (Supermarket Flyers, 7)

Fossils (Plastic Containers, 16)

Fringe T-Shirts (Fabric, 14)

Gingerbread People (Paper Bags, 2)

Grass Huts (Plastic Containers, 17)

Grocery Store Design (Supermarket Flyers, 2)

Hand Painted T-Shirts (Fabric, 16)

Hot-Air Balloon (Egg Cartons, 13)

Jigsaw Puzzle (Heavy Cardboard, 11)

Lacy Cedar Balls (Fabric, 11)

Leaf Hanging (Fabric, 6)

Leather-Look Vase (Miscellaneous, 23)

Letter Week (Newspaper, 6)

Log Houses (Newspaper, 5)

Message Holder (Miscellaneous, 14)

Mobiles (Plastic Berry Baskets, 8)

Moon Craters (Heavy Cardboard, 5)

Mouse (Paper Tubes, 3)

Mural (Miscellaneous, 28)

Nameplate (Egg Cartons, 11)

Nature Collages (Plastic Jar Lids, 11)

Nature Imprints (Plastic Containers, 1)

Nesting Baskets (Plastic Berry Baskets, 4)

Nests (Plastic Containers, 4)

Old Shoe Planter (Miscellaneous, 21)

Pail Planter (Plastic Containers, 23)

Paper Bag Stuffed Balloons (Paper Bags, 13)

Pebble Mosaic (Heavy Cardboard, 7)

Photo House (Wallpaper, 1)

Pie Tin Birdbath (Miscellaneous, 10)

Pinecone Bird Feeders (Miscellaneous, 12)

Place Value (Boxes, 7)

Planet Mural (Plastic Containers, 5)

Postage Stamp Flags (Miscellaneous, 22)

Print Making (Heavy Cardboard, 6)

Printing (Plastic Berry Baskets, 6)

Printing with Silly Putty (Newspaper, 8)

Puffy Paint on Fabric (Fabric, 1)

Rainbow Crayons (Miscellaneous, 3)

Relief Picture (Heavy Cardboard, 10)

Robots (Heavy Cardboard, 3)

Rolled Paper Beads (Paper Bags, 6)

Rolled Paper Sculptures (Paper Bags, 8)

Rubbings (Miscellaneous, 2)

Sand & Shell Collage (Heavy Cardboard, 2)

Sand Designs (Plastic Containers, 15)

Sand Layering (Plastic Containers, 3)

Sand Painting (Film Canisters, 9)

Scaly Pictures (Wallpaper, 4)

Seasonal Trees (Film Canisters, 5)

Shoebox Vehicles (Plastic Jar Lids, 6)

Soda Case Shadow Boxes (Boxes, 9)

Spiders (Plastic Containers, 11)

Sports Mural (Paper Bags, 10)

Spring Baskets (Plastic Berry Baskets, 1)

Spring Flowers (Egg Cartons, 8)

Starch Ghosts (Miscellaneous, 7)

Stone Creatures (Miscellaneous, 5)

Styrofoam Trees (Fabric, 5)

T-Shirt Pillows (Fabric, 9)

Tepees (Plastic Containers, 19)

Terrariums (Plastic Containers, 13)

Texture Collage (Wallpaper, 8)

Things About Me Wall Hanging (Paper Bags, 3)

Tie-Dye Painting (Fabric, 15)

Torn Paper Collage (Newspaper, 4)

Totem Poles (Paper Tubes, 4)

Tube People (Paper Tubes, 2)

Twig House (Miscellaneous, 11)

Vehicles (Heavy Cardboard, 4)

Visor (Plastic Containers, 7)

Wallpaper Clowns (Wallpaper, 7)

Watermelons (Miscellaneous, 20)

We Dress for Weather Dolls (Fabric, 4)

Weaving (Newspaper, 1)

Windsock (Paper Tubes, 6)

Word Collage (Newspaper, 2)